Learning Resource Centre

UXBRIDGE COLLEGE

Park Road, Uxbridge, Middlesex, UB8 1NQ

Renewals: 01895 853344

Please return this item to the LRC on or before the
last date stamped below:

658.31

PRESS

Alexandria, VA

ASTD Press is an internationally renowned source of insightful and practical information on workplace learning and performance topics, including training basics, evaluation and return-on-investment (ROI), instructional systems development (ISD), e-learning, leadership, and career development.

Ordering information: Books published by ASTD Press can be purchased by visiting our website at store.astd.org or by calling 800.628.2783 or 703.683.8100.

Library of Congress Control Number: 2006932488

ISBN-10: 1-56286-466-1
ISBN-13: 978-1-56286-466-8

ASTD Press Editorial Staff
Director: Cat Russo
Manager, Acquisitions & Author Relations: Mark Morrow
Editorial Manager: Jacqueline Edlund-Braun
Editorial Assistant: Kelly Norris

Editorial Contributor: Tad Simons
Copyeditor: Karen Eddleman
Proofreader: Kris Patenaude
Indexer: April Michelle Davis
Interior Design and Production: Kathleen Schaner
Cover Design and Illustration: Renita Wade
Cover Photographer: Sam Bortnick

Book printed by Victor Graphics, Inc., Baltimore, Maryland, www.victorgraphics.com.

Presentation Mastery, "So What Factor," Mr. Presentation, and 3-D Outline are registered trademarks of Tony Jeary High Performance Resources, LLC.

Contents

 # Preface

The book you hold in your hands represents a meeting of minds. That's because over the past two years, as the collaboration that resulted in this book unfolded, we discovered that we had more in common than just a first name (Tony). What became clear almost immediately after we met was that we share a vision of how the realms of business, communication, leadership, and learning ought to work—but don't.

From his vantage point at ASTD, Tony Bingham has a vision of elevating workplace learning to the point where it is a major strategic driver in every organization in the world. He also believes that learning professionals will play a central role in meeting the formidable challenges of the 21st-century global economy and that the profession needs to embrace those responsibilities now to shape and influence the future of workplace learning.

Tony Jeary is a communicator, presentation coach, and business strategist who has dedicated his professional life to Presentation Mastery, a set of principles and practices he developed in collaboration with Greg Kaiser and George Lowe. Anyone can use Presentation Mastery concepts to boost his or her professional success. In the course of his work, he has coached top executives in numerous *Fortune* 500 companies, including Ford, Samsung, Firestone, and Wal-Mart.

The goal of this book is to bring these two complementary world-views together—Tony Bingham's vision for workplace learning and Tony Jeary's principles of Presentation Mastery—to provide learning professionals of all kinds with a blueprint for managing the challenges ahead. Learning professionals who adopt the strategies for presenting learning initiatives outlined in this book are going to accelerate their own professional success and the success of others, and take giant strides toward revolutionizing how learning in the workplace is perceived, developed, and implemented in the coming years.

Why Focus on Communication?

Much of the frustration learning or training professionals encounter in their jobs stems from an inability to communicate the value of learning initiatives to the people who need to understand it the most: the executive-level decision makers. Certainly, many tools—simple and sophisticated—are available to evaluate learning programs and measure both the tangible and intangible results of every conceivable type of training. But, many measurement and evaluation efforts have been defensive in nature, and the impetus behind them seems to have been a rather desperate and ongoing battle to justify the next year's investment in workplace learning and to prevent people's jobs from disappearing. Many people in the field figured that once chief executive officers (CEOs) could see training's impact on the bottom line that the value of workplace learning would be self-evident.

Who Can Benefit from Reading This Book?

Whether your job title is trainer, workplace learning professional, training and development staff, HR member, chief learning officer (CLO), or human performance consultant, this book can help you understand your value and communicate it throughout your organization. Likewise, those in leadership positions can increase their understanding of how the learning function can make quantifiable and meaningful contributions to the organization, whether it's a corporation, a small business, a nonprofit, an academic institution, or a government entity. In the spirit of inclusiveness, we've used a variety of job titles interchangeably throughout *Presenting Learning*.

But, it isn't.

The problem is that the value of workplace learning is complex, multidimensional, hard to isolate, easy to underestimate, sometimes intangible, and often elusive. Its value is difficult to communicate in terse bullet points and definitive examples. For the past 20 years, the training and development profession has been preoccupied with quantifying every aspect of workplace learning, only to learn that the numbers don't tell the whole story; in fact, they can obscure or devalue the true story.

It's frustrating. Despite decades of research, reams of data, and dozens of different performance indexes and matrixes, communicating the value of training remains one of the major hurdles faced by the industry today. The one thing most people in the field of workplace learning and performance *haven't* learned how to do is persuasively, aggressively, and strategically present the case for learning *in language that CEOs understand, embrace, and feel compelled to act upon.*

It's not just about developing great programs and measuring outcomes; it's about managing expectations and communicating results in ways that top executives see as meaningful and impactful. It means speaking the language of business, not the language of trainers. Most important, it means making a direct connection between training and performance initiatives and the strategic objectives and key measures of the organization. In the past few years, many people have spoken of the importance of making just such a cause-and-effect link between training and the bottom line. *Presenting Learning* explains and illustrates specific strategies for accomplishing this crucial objective.

Just as numbers on a spreadsheet are not self-explanatory, the connection between a company's training initiatives and its strategic objectives is not always clear, and the results do not always speak for themselves. They need a voice—your voice—whether you are a trainer or a chief learning officer. Even then, it matters greatly who is hearing the message and how it is being interpreted. Most CEOs have similar general concerns, but they all think differently, they all have different specific challenges, and the politics inside every organization is unique.

To communicate with them in the most effective way possible—the way that is most likely to get them to sign off on your bold new initiatives—one must understand the entire context in which the conversation is taking place. This means understanding the company's goals and leaders, including their quirks, power struggles, successes, failures, leadership style, and business philosophy.

That's where Tony Jeary's principles of communication connect with the goals and aspirations of learning professionals. Tony Jeary is an expert at helping people shape their message for the audience and moment they are addressing. For the purposes of this book, he has agreed to share what he knows about communicating with top executives and to demonstrate how learning professionals can use his principles of communication mastery to present a more persuasive and compelling case for every initiative on the table. These principles aren't just for practitioners inside a company, either. They can just as easily be used by consultants and advisors who must get buy-in from the top before getting the go-ahead to work inside a company. Whether you are selling the value of training from inside or outside an organization, the key issue is still the same: What should you say and do to get the outcome you want?

A New Way of Thinking

It's a simple question, and it would be nice if the answer were just as straightforward, but it's not. If it were, you'd be reading a pamphlet, not a book.

Trainers are passionate about their profession. They believe wholeheartedly in the value of learning as a means for improving people's lives and careers, engaging employees, empowering people to reach their full potential, and improving the psychological and economic health of their organizations. This passion and belief in the power of learning is one of the great strengths that trainers bring to the corporate conversation. But, when it comes to actually getting things done, passion can lead to deadly blind spots. Many trainers believe so strongly in the value of their programs that they can't understand how anyone else could think otherwise. Consequently, many training and HR professionals, and even some CLOs, habitually approach discussions with upper management in an us-versus-them frame of mind. This is the sort of divisive attitude that, while understandable at times, usually is counterproductive. For one thing, it puts the disgruntled training advocate at a competitive disadvantage because it is an inherently defensive position. For another, it creates an artificial obstacle to overcome, because the fact is that there is no us-versus-them. In reality, there are just people in a room talking, working together to solve problems and accomplish something.

Meeting the Demands of the Future

Learning to work through organizational differences more effectively is important because learning professions are at an important crossroads. Once regarded as just another cog in the organizational wheel, most progressive companies now view "training" as an integral component of organizational success. In the March 2006 issue of *T&D,* management guru Tom Peters issued a bold challenge to the industry by declaring the war for respect from top management over. "Now what are you going to do?" he asked—and this is one of the questions we intend to answer.

Whether you agree with Peters, veterans in the industry can testify to the hard work and sacrifice necessary to get the ear of top executives. The effort has started to pay off: CLOs are now a common fixture in *Fortune* 500 executive suites, having earned that long-sought-after proverbial seat at the table of power. The workplace learning field is now its own discipline, with its own language and metrics. This has happened in large part because the transition from an industrial/worker economy to a knowledge/service economy has put a premium on workplace performance, development, learning, productivity, and retention—all areas that are directly affected by training. Economic developments in the past five years have also produced a confluence of needs that learning professionals are uniquely qualified to address. During the recession of 2001 and 2002, most companies had to cut back their workforces to stay competitive. Companies kept their best and most strategic-thinking people and "improved" their productivity by heaping more work on them. Now, companies are competitively leaner, but organizational growth is still an imperative. There is no magic formula for making this necessary growth happen. Terms such as "innovation," "creativity," "strategic thinking," and "organic growth" are bandied about, but at the end of the day someone has to have ideas and come up with a workable plan.

This is where the big opportunity lies for learning professionals. In many influential companies, such as IBM and Pfizer, workplace learning professionals are being asked to play an increasingly important role in shaping the strategic direction of their companies and developing the plans to make it happen. Why? According to a recent article in *Fortune* magazine, "After 500 years or so the scarcest, most valuable resource in business is no longer financial capital. It's talent.... Top talent has never been more valuable, nor competition for it more fierce" (Colvin, 2006). Of course, companies have been saying this for a long time, but the difference now is that they are starting to act like it. Increasingly, CEOs are recognizing that in a knowledge economy, the best defense against the competition is a knowledgeable, well-trained workforce that is smart enough to adapt to the evolving demands of the market on its own. Learning is no longer something people do once or twice a year to learn a job function; it's now an ongoing process that requires every employee to be able to work and learn at the same time, continuously updating his or her skills to meet the ever-changing demands of the modern workplace.

In such an environment, in any organization, learning professionals are the logical people to consult, so they must be ready when the call comes. It's also the learning professional's job to force the issue when the call *isn't* coming, but the needs for it clearly exist. We need to advocate for the use of workplace learning as a strategic business tool and to enlighten decision makers about the increasingly sophisticated ways in which learning is being used to drive business success and transform the 21st-century workplace.

Learning professionals aren't the only agents of change, of course. The unpredictable dynamics of an increasingly global economy are rapidly changing the ways in which companies and their leaders manage growth and respond to challenges. For example, the accelerating pace and volume of information available at any given time means that no one has all the information they need to make a correct decision. More and more, the most effective leaders in this new age of accelerated media are the ones who most effectively leverage their professional, social, and media networks, the ones who know how to convert the ideas and input from their best and brightest people into focused, decisive, visionary action.

In this time of exploding communication webs and extended global networks, workplace learning professionals are in the ideal position to help their organizations move forward. Every company needs its people to be united, organized, and energized by a vision of the future, and learning professionals are in the perfect position to help make those visions come true.

Presenting the Case for Learning

The purpose of this book is to teach you how to more effectively communicate what you already know is true: Workplace learning issues go to the heart of so many organizational functions and dysfunctions that no one would ignore or trivialize them. No company can completely do without training (though many have tried), so most companies are left with the question of what do *with* training.

That answer can come in many forms, however. Furthermore, *how* the training and learning function delivers those answers throughout the organization makes all the difference in how the message is received and whether learning programs will be implemented. The fact of the matter is that it's not enough to embrace a strategic leadership role, identify skills gaps, develop great programs, and measure results; you have to be able to do all that *and* communicate the value of what you are doing, effectively, persuasively—even inspirationally—to move the organization forward. Anything less results in mismanagement and frustration, all because you were unable to complete the final 20 percent of the equation for learning success: expertly presenting the case for learning when it counted the most.

Tony Bingham, as president and CEO of the American Society for Training & Development (ASTD), the world's largest association dedicated to workplace learning, focuses on helping learning professionals build their business acumen, understand the profession's role in addressing skills gaps, and connect their work to the strategic priorities and key measures of business leaders. His role in this book is to help you acquire the lexicon and skills necessary to understand the contributions of the learning function and to articulate the business case for learning more effectively by using an easy-to-remember, five-step model to guide you through the practical steps of the process.

To ensure that your most critical presentations achieve the results you're looking for, Tony Jeary explains how to apply the principles of Presentation Mastery—a proven model of expert presentation principles and practices—to the specific task of presenting learning initiatives, programs, and ideas in their best possible light.

We have also interviewed dozens of CEOs, CLOs, HR managers, and workplace learning professionals to find out what works when presenting learning initiatives to upper management. We've also put together numerous case studies on best practices that illustrate programs that were properly aligned with a business's strategic objectives and explain the methods for communicating the value of these programs for the purposes of securing executive-level buy-in and enterprisewide support. To make sure your presentation arsenal is complete, we've compiled a list of vital resources to help you pull together the information you need to make the strongest possible case for your own learning initiatives. Finally, to ensure you have information you can use immediately, we have created a concluding section for each chapter called "Very Important Points." This is your "take-away" action reminder to help you move one steep closer to becoming a valued strategic partner in your organization.

Looking into the Crystal Ball

The responsibilities of those accountable for organizational learning are undergoing a radical transformation in response to emerging realities of

A Bigger Picture

This isn't simply an instruction book on how to become a better presenter. If taken to heart, this book can change not only the way you think about your most critical presentations, but also the way you think about your job, your relationships with co-workers, and your overall role in the company or organization for which you work.

the global knowledge economy. Meeting future demands is going to require a different kind of workforce, one that is fast, nimble, flexible, efficient, and knowledgeable. Most important, the workforce of the future will be one that is constantly learning, assimilating what it knows, and then wanting—even demanding—to know more.

Because this workforce does not yet exist, much of the responsibility for creating it is going to fall on the shoulders of workplace performance and learning professionals. Therefore, it is their job to set the learning agenda for the 21st century. They must educate themselves as completely as possible about the realities and dynamics of doing business in the hyper-connected, information-saturated, on-demand workplace of the future. Armed with that knowledge, they can help their organizations make wise decisions that will lead down a rewarding path to prosperity.

Technology is not the key to this transformation, rather, communication, people, and new ideas are. Considering the stakes, you owe it to yourself and your organization to understand your value, serve as the best advocate for learning, and become the most effective presenter you can possibly be. It is our sincere hope that this book will help guide you toward this most worthwhile and necessary of goals.

Tony Bingham and Tony Jeary
April 2007

1

The New Reality of Workplace Learning

To the Point

The role of the workplace learning professional is evolving from that of a reactive producer of training programs and content to that of a proactive strategic planning partner responsible for understanding every aspect of the organization's business. Equipped with this knowledge, proactive learning professionals must develop and deploy learning solutions that address the organization's needs, support the organization's goals, deliver continuous value, and are intelligently integrated into the enterprise's processes, systems, and culture. That's a tall order, one that is going to require a new set of skills. This new skill set includes a firmer grasp of business and finance; a more strategic overall mindset about the learning profession; a greater awareness of and responsibility for creating one's own brand within an organization; and a recognition that presenting the value of training and learning is a daily challenge, not a once- or twice-a-year event.

Everyone knows the drill. The economy starts to go south, costs need to be contained, and the organization needs to be right sized. Usually the first budget on the chopping block is the training budget. Next up are any outside consultants, coaches, or vendors deemed unnecessary to the organization's survival, followed by marketing people, human resources staff, and seemingly anyone else whose primary responsibility involves people rather than numbers.

It always comes as a bit of a shock. Developing people, making them more productive, giving them rewarding work, pulling them together as a team: Shouldn't these be top organizational priorities, during good times and bad? Most executives take great pride in their organization's ability to nurture the extraordinary talent that makes their company successful. They also acknowledge that if they want to remain competitive, people are a key investment because they bring value to the bottom line, which is something all the organization's stakeholders can applaud. Why does all that seem to go out the window when belt-tightening is called for? Obviously, there's a disconnect here.

The Communication Chasm

Miscommunication is what causes so many tears to be shed in the learning profession. It's also why we decided to write this book. Something is happening in such situations that goes far beyond a simple lack of communication. After all, chief executive officers (CEOs) and other top executives are reasonable, intelligent people, and so are learning professionals, executive coaches, and others who make their living advising organizations on how to be more successful. These parties should be able to talk to each other; and when times are good and the money is flowing, they often see eye-to-eye on many things, including the undeniable value of all sorts of training. Under different circumstances, however, with different pressures and factors in play, these two important sides of the organizational coin can often seem to be speaking entirely different languages. In these situations, mutual understanding disintegrates, communication fractures, frustration builds, arguments ensue; and the executives, who have the trump card of power on their side, usually get their way.

Why does this happen? And, what needs to change to break this frustrating cycle?

First, let's clear up a few misconceptions. No, the CEO hasn't lost his or her marbles. No, the rest of the executive team isn't filled with trainer-hating members. And, no, the training function isn't any less valuable to an organization when times are tough than when times are good. So what's the *real* problem?

We believe that the friction that may exist between an organization's upper management and its training functions—whether they are administered internally, externally, or both—is not just a garden-variety breakdown in communication. Rather, it's a very specific type of communication lapse, one with identifiable causes, proven remedies, and a high probability of being successfully overcome if you are willing to do the work necessary to make it happen.

The program we are going to outline for you in this book will certainly help you get the job done, but the responsibility for success is ultimately going to fall on your shoulders. This may not be what you want to hear. You may be thinking: If the powers that be—those top decision makers—would only open their minds a little, they would understand the value learning brings to the table. This is true, except that it's not their responsibility to open their own minds; it's your responsibility to help them see the value of learning, it is your job to help them understand what they are sacrificing when they shortchange the learning function, and it is up to you to make sure they "get" the depth and breadth of learning's contribution. Then, the next time the economic pendulum swings, they will know, quantifiably, that cutting the training budget is not the way to save money for the overall organization.

Wouldn't It Be Great?

Wouldn't it be great to have a CEO who understands the value of learning so well that you never even have to fight this fight again? To have a CEO who is so supportive of the learning function that the value it adds to the organization is never questioned? To have a CEO who is actually learning's biggest cheerleader? One who puts so much stock in training that he or she bets the company's own stock on it?

It can and does happen. And you don't need a master's degree in business administration to do it; you just need to understand what the root causes of the miscommunication are, work hard to address them, have the right information available when it is needed, present it in a way that ensures buy-in from all stakeholders, and do the appropriate follow-up and follow-through necessary to keep your end of the bargain.

A Role in Flux

Like it or not, if you are trying to persuade top-tier decision makers that your department, programs, or both bring value to the organization, it is ultimately your responsibility to show them how. They shouldn't have to speculate and wonder. Fortunately, that's precisely

After reading this book, you'll better know how to:

- Communicate more strategically with upper-executive decision makers.
- Present the business case for learning more persuasively.
- Position yourself as an organization's strategic partner, not just a service provider.
- Talk about value of training in language business executives understand and respect.
- Make the intangible tangible.
- Tell a compelling story with numbers and statistics.
- Generate support for current and future workplace learning initiatives throughout the organization.
- Sell your services more effectively, particularly if you're an outside consultant, coach, or vendor.
- Serve your organization so well that management will want to promote you, not fire you.

what CEOs and their management teams want to hear. They *want* to know if the programs they have already approved are getting the job done. They *want* to know how future programs, initiatives, and solutions are going to affect the bottom line. They *need* to know the degree to which their training and performance improvement efforts are moving the organization's strategies forward. If there is a better, more effective, and efficient way to achieve the same objectives (outsourcing some services, say), they want to know about that, too.

Furthermore, today's CEOs need learning professionals' help more than ever. That's because a rare convergence of economic, political, technological, and sociological factors has put learning professionals front and center in the ongoing struggle to initiate and sustain positive, productive, progressive change in organizations worldwide. A tremendous opportunity exists for learning professionals everywhere to expand their contribution to these organizations and, along with it, their influence and power.

Of course, what's really happened is that many companies have exhausted all the quick and easy ways to boost productivity, and now they must find other innovative ways to grow. Faced with directors and shareholders who still want to see a healthy return to the bottom line, CEOs must continue to improve organizational performance through new products, services, and ideas that are skillfully developed and executed by people who are well prepared for the job.

That's where workplace learning comes into play. Learning professionals are responsible for making sure that people in an organization are properly skilled and that the enterprise is staffed with the best-equipped people. Ensuring that all of them are trained to support the organization's goals as effectively and efficiently as possible is a key responsibility for the profession. Because corporate decision makers are focused primarily on growth and understand that people, well prepared, are their key advantage, many are eager to see what learning professionals can do for them. Getting the most and best out of the talent in their organizations has become a top priority. So the learning and performance improvement function of many companies now is expected to spearhead the next wave of significant growth. It's a huge responsibility, and if learning professionals in the field are equal to the task, it could be a momentous turning point that the profession has been seeking since it started. We must deliver.

Unfortunately, the results of workplace learning efforts so far have not been as impressive as one might hope. In June 2006, Accenture published the results of its latest High Performance Workforce Study, which it conducts every 18 months. Two hundred fifty senior executives were surveyed about the learning function in their organizations. Only 10 percent of the respondents reported being "very satisfied" with their human resources and training. Only 14 percent said they had an industry-leading workforce. And even though the most influential thinkers in our industry have been preaching the importance of aligning performance initiatives with an organization's strategic objectives, only 20 percent of the respondents agreed that most of their employees understand their companies' strategic objectives and know what is necessary to be successful in their industry.

Conclusion: Although some companies are effectively using their HR and learning departments as a strategic driver of organizational goals, most organizations do not have their act together when it comes to the role of training and workforce development. Furthermore, most workplace learning professionals have yet to convince their senior management that learning should be integrated into the organization's strategic planning and to implement programs and practices that are satisfying top executives. And learning professionals have little to provide in the way of data that demonstrates learning's contribution to organizational results and how learning initiatives are linked to organizational strategies.

A New Set of Skills and a Transformed Mindset

A 2006 Accenture workforce study points out what some would call a big problem, but we look at it as an opportunity and a challenge (Accenture 2006). Senior executives who are expecting great things out of their learning initiatives are giving learning professionals a prime opportunity to prove what they've been preaching all these years: that time, money, faith, and effort spent on training and performance improvement initiatives are a wise investment. The challenge, of course, is for proactive learning professionals to deliver meaningful, compelling results translated into metrics that senior management understands and cares about, metrics that prove that learning initiatives are aligned with organizational results and strategies.

Not only must learning professionals produce business-level results critical in today's cautious business climate, but they also must be able to *continually communicate the value of those results to the enterprise and learn how to build incrementally on their successes.* This means developing a new set of skills, ones honed specifically for the task of talking persuasively and presenting the case for learning in ways that influential decision makers find compelling enough to support the learning function regardless of the economic climate. That's why a major focus of this book is on presentation skills and strategies that can help learning professionals earn and keep that coveted seat at the boardroom table.

Workplace learning professionals, executive coaches, business consultants, and training suppliers all struggle against skeptical executives, organizational inertia, entrenched bureaucracies, employees who don't want to be trained, managers who think they already know better, and intractable mindsets of every type. But we don't think unenlightened CEOs and upper executives are necessarily the problem; when asked, most CEOs say that training is an extremely important component of their organization, one they take very seriously. Yet, when it comes to prioritizing the cost of this eminently worthwhile activity, training is rarely a top priority, so its budgets are vulnerable. This seemingly inexplicable phenomenon is a source of frustration for anyone who needs to cultivate support from the top—support that is crucial to successful training initiatives.

The problem in such cases is not necessarily a lack of evidence that training is working. You can have binders full of data and dozens of examples of how training has benefited the organization and still run into resistance at any level of the organization. To the well-meaning learning professional, this resistance may seem illogical, but it is resistance nonetheless, and the only way to fight it is to understand what's behind it.

Are We Communicating Yet?

Communication is a tricky thing, and one of the tricks it plays on professionals at all levels is the illusion that it's really happening. It often isn't. The true problem is rarely what it appears to be on the surface. If a CEO asks a question about return-on-investment (ROI), for instance, it could be a simple request for a number, but, more likely, it is a probe for something else. Among the possibilities are the following:

- information to help him or her understand training's effect on the organization as a whole
- reassurance that training is making a difference somehow
- evidence that the company's money and energy are going in the right places
- clues about issues that need to be addressed in the future
- a sense of the resources that are going to be available in the coming year
- knowledge about how effectively and efficiently the organization's current programs are running
- a test to see how well you understand a program's systemic influence on the organization
- a feeler to make sure the program itself supports specific organizational objectives.

In short, a seemingly simple question from a corporate-level executive could be motivated by dozens of different factors, none of which are self-evident. If you are the one being asked to answer the question, however, you are also being asked to answer the question *beneath* the question—the core issue that the voiced question may be masking. In the game of corporate communication, if you recognize the issues informing the question and can address them directly in your answer, you are seen as someone who can cut through the clutter and get to the point. You are also recognized for knowing your organization well enough to perceive what the issues on the table really are and having the wherewithal to answer them directly and thoroughly.

However, if you *don't* understand where a question is coming from or can't deduce the true motivator behind a question—that is, if you take the question merely at face value—your answer is likely to be off target. The person to whom you are speaking is likely to know it, and the communication between you may start to unravel. Rather than experiencing your answer as an insightful, on-target assessment that goes directly to the important aspect, the CEO will experience your answer as a rambling, insufficient stab at answering the surface question only.

At the same time, without knowing why, you will begin to feel while you are talking that the CEO's interest in what you are saying is being withdrawn gradually. You won't know why the CEO's attention has drifted, so you won't know what to do to get it back. You'll soldier on, doing the best you can, but you may not be rewarded with the results you were seeking. For some bizarre, mystifying reason that you can't quite put your finger on, your words will have convinced no one, and your efforts will have been in vain. In the end, you'll be one of the legions of learning professionals and consultants frustrated that no matter what evidence they produce to support their cause and no matter how eloquently they defend it, their arguments are ignored.

People usually talk about such experiences in vague terms, saying things such as they "weren't on the same wavelength," or they "didn't see eye-to-eye," or they "just weren't connecting," all of which are true. Part of what we are trying to explain to you, the reader, is why such miscommunications happen, what you need to do to prevent them, and how to turn what was once a communication obstacle into a powerful strategic advantage.

We believe that Tony Jeary's Presentation Mastery program addresses the roots of most communication problems that plague business professionals. What the Presentation Mastery approach offers learning professionals is an arsenal of communication strategies and techniques that can transform the way you do your job and, in the process, position you as a potent agent of change and valuable strategic asset to any organization. In addition, you'll learn how to brand yourself as a leader in both thought and action—as someone who sees farther over the competitive horizon, is better connected to the competitive realities facing the organization, and whose input and insight are extremely valuable. In short, you'll learn how to develop the respect and power necessary to influence top decision makers, get them to buy into the programs and initiatives you propose, and help them understand the wisdom and value of making learning a permanent part of the organization's strategic core.

Connecting the Dots, Communicating Value

Another pervasive challenge faced by learning professionals, one that causes a host of communication problems, is connecting the dots between an organization's stated strategies and objectives, training programs that support those objectives, and tangible results that demonstrate the effectiveness of a given training program or solution.

Learning professionals often fixate on such evaluation tools as Kirkpatrick's four levels of training evaluation (Kirkpatrick & Kirkpatrick, 2005), Jack Phillips's (2003) ROI measurement methods, training management system reports, and other means of measuring training's impact on the job or organization. These are all important processes to go through and the information collected from them can be extremely valuable, but only if you know what to do with it. Too many learning professionals expend extraordinary amounts of energy gathering various statistics and evaluation materials but drop the ball when it comes to strategically using that information to get what they want.

The truth is that communicating one's value in meaningful ways is imperative for survival. Those who can't explain how or why they are valuable in terms that the questioner can understand and embrace risk being eliminated. The questions that vex learning professionals aren't ones of why, but of how: How do I communicate the value of something I have difficulty measuring? How do I convince people that this program is vital, necessary, and potentially profitable? How do I convince management to spend money on measurement and metrics? How can I get the performance and HR functions to have the same level of clout and respect as other business units? If coaching in leadership or presentation skills, for example, cannot be tied directly to a profit number, how can I convince this organization that I am a consultant worth hiring?

To answer those questions, we have devised a simple five-part strategy—the SPEAK model—for more effectively analyzing, articulating, and initiating learning in any organization. Aligning learning with the strategic objectives of the organization is the key. The only way to do that effectively is to take a proactive approach to the learning function. Learning professionals need to be setting the agenda, not reacting to it. By taking the offensive and accepting responsibility for making learning an indispensable component of the organization's success, learning professionals will naturally open doors that used to be closed, and new opportunities for contribution will present themselves.

Following the model, you will develop your own strategies for handling whatever specific situations or challenges confront you in your own organization or with the clients you serve. When you are trying to convince someone to support and believe in the value that well-developed and executed training can deliver—when you are *presenting learning,* that is—diligently pursuing these five steps can be your own greatest strategic asset. Likewise, failing to follow through in these five areas can cause a great deal of frustration, anxiety, and, possibly, failure. Whether you embrace them as tools to help you communicate the value of what you are doing or just use them as guidelines to help you do your job more effectively, they are essential for surviving and thriving in the 21st-century organization. They also happen to be good for business because, by using them, you naturally end up doing what's best for the health and welfare of the organization, which benefits everyone.

New Strategies. New Ideas. Better Results.

It is our belief that by adopting the principles of Presentation Mastery and applying them to the five-part SPEAK model for strategic alignment of training with the organization's business goals, learning professionals of all kinds will find the keys to success they've been searching for. Our goal is to provide you with a powerful new set of strategies, techniques, and tools to overcome the most frequent obstacles that stand in your way as a learning professional. It doesn't matter what level of the career ladder you're on—a newly hired trainer or a seasoned chief learning officer (CLO)—the same basic principles can be adapted for any position and can help anyone serve his or her organization or clients better.

In most cases, these aren't skills unfamiliar to you. For example, many trainers are justifiably proud of their overall presentation skills and believe that they are at their best in front of a room. And this may be true. But that doesn't necessarily mean they are using their formidable skills as strategically as possible, with their own specific goals and objectives in mind, and applying their presentation skills in ways that ensure the most favorable possible outcome. On the flip side, excellent presentation skills can be a liability if they lull people into a false sense of confidence and lead them to dismiss the need for proper preparation. Many a cocky executive has gone into a presentation, winged it, and thought he did great because he survived with his dignity and reputation intact only to find that the outcome wasn't quite what he wanted or expected.

We've called the book *Presenting Learning*, but you will soon find that it's not just a book about giving presentations about learning. It's also a book that will encourage you to begin thinking about your job, as well as your overall role in the conversation of corporate ideas, in exciting, energizing new ways. Learning professionals are on the cusp of one of the most exciting transformations in business history. Over the next 20 years, almost everything companies do will change to accommodate the demands of a global network of business relationships that transcend geography, politics, language, and time. The only thing that will remain constant during this period will be the need to teach the workers, leaders, and innovators how to adapt to their changing world and perform at their very best. That's the learning professional's job, one of the most important and rewarding jobs in the world. That's never going to change, but *how* the job is done *will* change. Working effectively in this new environment means embracing a model for aligning and integrating the training and learning function with the goals, vision, and metrics of the organization in much more conscious and deliberate ways than you probably ever have before. If you're already working this way, with these goals in mind, that's great; we hope you'll pick up some valuable pointers that will help you do your job even better. If not, our goal is that this book will offer a cohesive strategic plan for learning professionals who are struggling with the myriad challenges they are suddenly facing and who are looking for more effective ways to make a difference in their organizations.

One thing is for sure: In the coming years, CLOs, trainers, consultants, and HR personnel everywhere are going to be charged with the task of transforming their companies and clients into the sort of sophisticated, agile, responsive, learning-centered organizations that really work. All this talk about shifting global realities and organizational transformation may sound a bit radical, and that's because it is. We didn't write this book to provide you with a bunch of great presentation tips; we wrote it because organizations in the 21st century are facing unprecedented global challenges, and the speed, agility, intelligence, and creativity with which we address them is of the utmost importance. In a knowledge economy influenced by enormous generational shifts in intellectual capital as well as vast demographic shifts that are changing social landscapes and economies all over the world, learning professionals are in the thick of it. If we've done our job right, the following pages will help guide you into this new role as a tireless agent of meaningful and measurable change and champion of learning and help make the journey one that is satisfying, rewarding, and profitable for everyone.

Very Important Points

- Workplace learning professionals must take responsibility for helping executives understand the true value of learning and the contribution it makes to the success of the enterprise.

- Because top management relies on the performance improvement and learning functions to spearhead the next wave of organizational growth, those working in the field of learning must help their management teams make the most of the organization's talent.

- Learning professionals must learn to deliver meaningful results that senior management can embrace, translated into metrics and language they care about.

- Lack of data is not the only reason learning professionals, coaches, and consultants fail to overcome resistance from upper executives. One big reason is a lack of understanding about where resistance is coming from and why.

- When CEOs ask a question, often it is the question *behind the question* that matters most. Address it, and you will get the respect you deserve.

- The Presentation Mastery principles, combined with the five-step SPEAK plan for managing and implementing learning in a strategic, proactive fashion, represent a powerful new set of skills, techniques, and tools for learning professionals who want to take their position and profession to the next level.

In this chapter, you've learned about the importance of being able to communicate the value of learning during good times and bad. The next chapter provides an in-depth look at the Presentation Mastery principles that can provide a framework for presenting learning to your organization's executives.

2

The Magic of the Presentation Mastery Approach

To the Point

The changing role of learning and performance professionals requires developing a greater set of skills. Learning's increasingly important role in business strategy and organizational effectiveness involves a far more practical understanding of sales, marketing, and persuasion than traditional learning roles. The common thread that runs through this new skill set is the importance of communication and presentation skills. The Presentation Mastery approach is a collection of best-practice communication principles that allows people to position themselves as levers of influence in an organization, as well as proactive agents of change. The magic lies in being better prepared to communicate one's ideas, better able to recognize new opportunities and take advantage of them, and being equipped with the skill and confidence to leverage the benefits of operating at the highest possible level of communication effectiveness.

Why Should You Care?

Why should anyone in the field of workplace learning worry about improving his or her presentation and communication effectiveness? After all, if you are in this business, you have doubtless delivered hundreds of presentations and are quite good at it by now. You may even pride yourself on your presentation ability and believe it's one of your biggest professional strengths. You've cracked tough audiences, had them laughing in the aisles, enjoyed commanding a group's attention, and have already digested all the public-speaking advice you can swallow. Why more? Why now?

The presentation and communication side of learning is so important that a book needed to be written about it. The world is changing, and learning professionals need to change with it. The expanding global economy is exerting greater pressure on companies to get the most out of their people in terms of greater efficiency, creativity, leadership, loyalty, and business acumen. For companies, the ultimate goal is to fuel growth and feed the bottom line. Increasingly, CEOs and their teams are coming to the conclusion that those goals are impossible unless their people are adequately trained and prepared for their roles in the organization, and that's the job of learning professionals who have been training people for decades. The difference now is that the pressure is on for the learning function to make a much more significant contribution than it has in the past.

Many of the most respected and profitable companies are setting the performance bar ever higher. CLOs at such companies as IBM, Pfizer, Hewlett-Packard, Johnson Controls, Caterpillar, Black & Decker, and dozens of others are transforming the way their organizations approach the whole idea of workplace learning. The notion of training departments serving up "canned" courses and content is rapidly giving way to a new era in which the learning function of an organization operates as a fully empowered partner working with upper management to deploy learning solutions that serve and support the organization's strategic objectives and drive its key metrics. In such environments, a direct, measurable connection between a company's learning practices and overall goals is mandatory. Learning's contribution to the organization can't be assumed; it must be tangible and provable, with supporting statistics and other metrics that can be tracked over time. Workplace learning must make business sense, and those making the business case for learning must know how to communicate it. They must also be capable of persuading upper management that what they are doing is having a positive impact on the organization as a whole, is continually improving the organization's ability to compete in its market, and is the most effective means of managing the organization's knowledge and talent.

The Challenge: Survival in the 21st Century

The connecting thread of all of these new demands on the learning function is accountability to upper management. Learning professionals have never had to justify their existence more strenuously or prove their value to the organization more convincingly. Persuasion and sales skills are becoming an increasingly important part of the job. Knowledge of business and finance is also a job requirement. Daily interaction with upper management and other departments is occurring more often, requiring more cross-functional communication of all types. A premium is also put on leadership skills because getting a CEO, three vice presidents, six department heads, and a battalion of line workers to agree on the importance of a strategic, companywide learning initiative is a far different challenge from simply generating the courses and content the boss wants.

To meet this challenge, learning professionals need a set of communication strategies, skills, techniques, and tools that allow them to shine in the more demanding roles that await them. Those who develop the requisite knowledge, communication skills, and business acumen will survive and thrive in the competitive marketplace of the 21st century. Those who don't, won't.

Tony Jeary's Solution: Presentation Mastery Principles

The Presentation Mastery concept was developed by coauthor Tony Jeary as a way of consolidating everything he knew about the art of giving presentations into a package of ideas that others could use to improve. One of the most important secrets to delivering great presentations is not thinking about them the way other people do. Most people think of presentations as events that happen at a specific time and that have definite parts: before (preparation), during (presentation delivery), and after (follow-up). This, unfortunately, is not a productive way to think about presentations at all. In fact, thinking about presentations as independent events that must be prepped for, agonized over, and obsessed about is precisely why so many people hate and fear them. Thinking about presentations in this way often generates the anxiety that people associate with public speaking. It also can cause people to develop bad habits and can undermine just about everything they are trying to accomplish, such as connecting with the audience, getting their message across, being persuasive, appearing professional, and impressing everyone in the room.

A much better way to think about presentations is that they are one form of communication among many and that they are happening around you all the time in the form of phone calls, emails, conversations with colleagues, casual meetings, and so forth. Most forms of business communication have an element of presentation in them. Leaving someone a voicemail message is a kind of mini-presentation. Sending an email is a written presentation of sorts. Chance encounters and spontaneous conversations with people in the course of the business day are also forms of presentation, especially if you are trying to get something done and need to influence people's thoughts and behaviors to make it happen.

What Is a Presentation?

A presentation is the act of working to change the content of another person's mind at a particular time and place. By adopting the philosophy that presentations can happen any time, anywhere, you open up a whole world of presentation possibilities. Think about your own professional life. How often do you converse or interact with people in the course of a day, and how often are those interactions connected in at least some small way to getting your job done and moving the organization forward? If you ask most people how many presentations they give in a week, they will usually answer "none," "one," or "a few," depending on their job. But, if you consider all of the other types of presentation-related communications you have in a week, what's the number? Dozens? Hundreds? If you think of all of these interactions as types of presentations, at least two things become immediately apparent: First, the day is filled with opportunities for people to work on their presentation skills, and, second, the big, "important" presentations don't seem quite so daunting, because they are simply big, blown-up versions of what one does every day.

The average learning professional gives more presentations than most, but they all break down into about 10 different types of presentations:

1. general training sessions (orientation, self-improvement, or general management skills training)

2. training seminars (intense, topic-specific sessions with 10 to 1,000 people)

3. learning presentations (videoconferences, online classes)

4. meetings (in person or on the phone); speeches (talks that don't involve training)

5. sales presentations (business development or program pitches)

6. facilitated events (workgroups or other programs to help people work together in some way)

7. one-on-one (in person or on the phone)

8. electronic presentations (faxes, emails, electronic bulletin boards, or PowerPoint presentations)

9. branding messages (communicating what you stand for as an organization or a person)

10. media presentations (press interviews—radio, television, or print).

Each of these different types of presentations has different goals and expectations, and each requires a slightly different set of skills and a different approach, *if* the overall goal is to make the most of every encounter.

One big difference between the average presenter and a Presentation Master is that the average person sees all of these communications as separate events that happen here and there with no real connection other than being physically present at them is part of the job. A Presentation Master, however, views them as intimately linked events connected by an overall strategy and a message that the Master has consciously decided upon. Each event is an opportunity to execute that strategy and reinforce that message. Rather than checking off a list of individual activities during the day, a person operating according to the principles of Presentation Mastery sees them all as small communication steps leading to a much larger goal—communicating a strategic, cohesive, consistent message that feeds into everything else he or she is doing.

Consequently, the Presentation Master's day has a feel of flow, focus, and purpose, whereas the average person's day just feels like an exhausting string of sessions and meetings. How often have you thought to yourself, "I was going to get something done today, but the day ended up getting eaten by a bunch of meetings and little fires that needed to be put out?" This rarely happens to people operating at the Presentation Mastery level because they realize that all communication events offer a chance to advance toward their larger goals in some way. It may be a small step—maybe even one that most people wouldn't recognize as a step—but it is a step forward nonetheless. Thus, their professional lives have a sense of momentum; they don't waste time; they know what they want and how to get it; they make things happen. They are the sort of people companies want to employ because, besides knowing how to get things done, they are also highly self-motivated and tend to gravitate toward leadership positions. They are action-oriented, get-it-done people, not necessarily because they are smarter than everyone else or have more talent, but because how they think informs the way they act in a way that creates a self-perpetuating cycle of success. To the outsider they may seem like lucky people who get lots of breaks, but the truth is that because they look at things with a larger perspective, they see more opportunities and are often able to act on them before other people recognize them as such. It's an everyday competitive advantage that, over time, accelerates their success and makes them formidable opponents as well as valuable allies.

Mastery Magic

The magic of Presentation Mastery really means working and thinking in ways that make good fortune happen. Such instances may materialize out of nowhere, often from a chance encounter or short conversation, and are usually unpredictable except that they always happen because of an openness to serendipity and a willingness to walk through the door of opportunity when it opens.

Presentation Masters do this all the time. Not only do they recognize the connections between their scheduled and unscheduled presentations, but also they leverage the unexpected opportunities that arise in those chance interactions, make the most of serendipitous circumstances and connections, and have the awareness and wherewithal to see how the pieces fit together in the big picture. In the office, this might mean recognizing how two people in different departments complement each other and then having them collaborate on a project. As a consultant from the outside, it might mean connecting pieces of conversation with a chief financial officer to similar work you did for a client three years ago, or noticing the CEO's fly-fishing hat on a shelf and using a fishing analogy to illustrate a point. Whatever the circumstance, the process amounts to putting two or more details together to open up a possibility that didn't exist before. Good conversationalists

When Opportunity Knocks, Can You Hear It?

The ability to see opportunities and spontaneously act on them is similar in principle to some of the ideas explored in Malcolm Gladwell's (2005) book *Blink: The Power of Thinking Without Thinking,* which describes leaders who rely on their gut feelings to make fast, accurate decisions, as opposed to people who tend to amass great quantities of information and digest it all before making a decision. Tony Jeary recalls an incident not long ago that illustrates how this *Blink*-like, opportunity-knocking mechanism works in the mind of a Presentation Master:

"One day last summer I was going over some papers when the phone rang. Turned out it was someone from a company that sells outdoor lighting wanting to know if I was interested in buying some lights for my house. He mumbled a quick introduction, but I didn't quite catch the name of the company and he was obviously a bit nervous about calling. He seemed more interested in ending the phone call than making a sales pitch, and I could have easily just said, 'No, I'm not interested,' and hung up. Instead, I said, 'No, I'm not interested in any lights, but you should really consider hiring me to help *your* company because your sales approach, message, and delivery style aren't going to convince *anyone* in my neighborhood to buy *anything* from you.' The man on the phone turned out to be the president of the company, and he admitted that sales weren't going particularly well, which was why he was the one working the phones. I invited him over to see what my team could do for him.

"In less than four hours, we completely rebranded his company, giving it an evocative name (Creative Nightscapes) and a tagline ('Painting your home with light') to reflect what the company did in terms that would resonate emotionally with potential customers. My designer whipped up a brochure and some business cards, and we wrote him a short elevator speech to use when approaching prospects. About a month later, I received a check for $30,000, along with an offer to outfit my home with lights free. The enclosed note told the story: Sales had boomed. Now he had more work than he knew what to do with and was starting to hire more people to handle his business's expansion.

"The point of this story is not that I'm such an awesome presenter that I can make $30,000 every time I pick up the phone. The point is that most people see telemarketers as a nuisance and reflexively say 'No, thanks' when they call. In this particular instance, however, because business branding and strategy are part of the package of services that my company provides, I saw an opportunity. Here was a man obviously in need of some help marketing his business, and that's the sort of need my business fills. I was able to intuit his need and offer him a solution on the spot. The opportunity to spin it that way and put the conversation into an entirely different context, one in which I was offering *him* a service, lasted only a few seconds, but I took advantage of that moment and both our companies ended up with a win."

do this sort of connecting instinctively. For example, they might ask someone where he's from:

"Dallas, Texas," he'll say.

"My brother-in-law lives in Plano and works for Texas Instruments."

"No kidding. I worked at TI for five years."

"Do you know so-and-so?"

Pretty soon a connection is established and the two parties are putting together threads of connection.

The difference between someone who is a good conversationalist and someone who is exercising some degree of Presentation Mastery is that the conversationalist is probably only making connections to keep the conversation going. The Presentation Master, however, is asking questions with a conscious strategy in mind and is placing each answer in the context of an action plan that he or she is already pursuing, perhaps on multiple fronts. If the person to whom the Master is talking fits into that plan somehow, the Master will identify how and find a way to make productive use of that connection. It's not as cold and calculating as it sounds, though, because much of the Master's energy also goes into helping other people pursue and achieve their goals. These favors are inevitably returned, pulling Masters along on a tide of goodwill.

Life Is a Series of Presentations

Almost every form of communication is a type of presentation. If you have done your homework and competently handled the hundreds of small presentation opportunities—impromptu conversations, short meetings with co-workers, phone calls, emails, and so forth—then you have laid a foundation for success when larger presentations arise. Ideas converge, goals come together, there are no unfortunate surprises, you are in complete control, and—as if by magic—you are able to focus the energy in the room on supporting your own goals and objectives, and on paving a strategically decisive road to future action (Jeary, Dower, & Fishman, 2004). The reason things happen this way for those who practice the principles of Presentation Mastery is that they are operating in level 3 of the presentation impact curve (figure 2-1).

In the presentation world, most people operate at levels 1 or 2, where the impact of their presentations improves steadily as they acquire basic delivery skills and they learn how to interact with an audience. Most people are also content to settle for "good enough" presentation skills to get by, even though high-performing professionals all over the world insist that good presentation skills are the means to accelerate an individual's success.

Figure 2-1. The presentation impact curve.

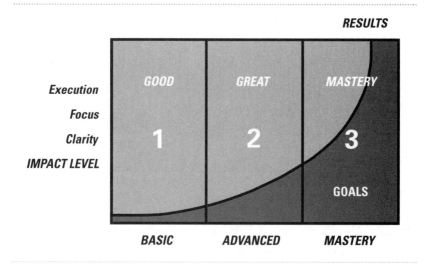

Now, you'll notice that something interesting happens to the impact curve between level 2 and level 3: All of a sudden, incremental improvements start to yield exponential results. Salespeople, for instance, instead of having a 20 or 30 percent closing rate start closing sales at a rate of 80 or 90 percent. People who were merely effective in their jobs are suddenly unstoppable. Their confidence soars, their results skyrocket, doors open for them, and these people can look forward to a better future.

The reason this exponential acceleration of results happens is that people who are operating at a high level of communication Mastery are disciplined users of advanced process and communication techniques that *effectively ensure that they achieve their presentation and communication objectives almost 100 percent of the time.* These people do the same things as others—they take phone calls, meet with clients, banter with colleagues in the lunchroom, make both informal and formal presentations, and so on. The difference is that whenever a Master is communicating, *he or she knows how to say the right thing, at the right time, to the right people—in a way that ensures that the Master's short-term goals are met and the foundation for meeting his or her long-term goals has been laid.*

Small Improvements = Big Differences

The other principle at work at level 3 on the impact curve is that very few people operate at that level of expertise, so small differences in ability can yield disproportionately large dividends. If two highly qualified candidates for CEO are competing, the difference that gives one the edge over the other may be small, but, all other things being equal, that tiny difference ends up being everything. Those who operate as if their life is a series of presentations and structure their working life to reflect this fact create more opportunities for themselves, put themselves in a position to take advantage of those opportunities, and, like cyclists who find their second wind, start pulling away from the pack.

The good news for anyone working in the field of learning and performance is that most of you are already communicating at level 2 on the presentation impact curve. You are already comfortable in front of a crowd, have command of your material most of the time, and would rate your presentation skills as "pretty good." That means most of you are perfectly poised to make the jump to level 3 and start earning the dividends of Mastery.

The Learning Pro's Presentation Universe

No matter where your skill level puts you on the presentation impact curve, the first step toward Mastery is defining your presentation universe. As mentioned earlier, a learning professional's work involves about 10 basic types of presentations (listed earlier in this chapter), ranging from impromptu telephone calls to companywide events with hundreds or thousands of people. Your presentation universe is a detailed breakdown of the number and type of presentations you give in a typical day, week, or month. Most people, when they do this exercise, begin by thinking that they give a few presentations a week at most. But, when they expand their awareness of what a presentation really is, they realize that they engage in hundreds of interactions every week in which they are trying to influence another person's thoughts or actions. Try your hand at completing the template for your presentation universe in figure 2-2. How many did you count?

Now that you've defined your presentation universe, ask yourself two questions: How many of these communication opportunities are you truly prepared for? And, how often do these interactions result in the outcome you desire? During the day, for example, do you find yourself incrementally achieving your goals and objectives and feeling energized by the forward momentum of your efforts? Or, do you feel as if you are constantly running around, going to meetings, putting out fires, being interrupted 50 times a day, and getting nothing done? Does your workday feel structured and purposeful? Or, does it feel like a haphazard chain of frenetic events over which you have little or no control?

You might think of the difference as an issue of time management, organization, or dysfunctional leadership—and you wouldn't necessarily be wrong about that—but notice also that what we're talking about here are two different frames of mind, two different *ways of thinking* while on

Figure 2-2. An example of a presentation universe for a workplace learning professional.

Name:

Presentation Universe

What	Rating	Times per Year	Number of Participants	Duration	Description/Opportunity	Actions
Training Session	7	100	5-100	1-8 hr	Train on various subjects	Open with clear objectives.
Staff Meeting	5	50	3-10	60 min	Weekly staff meeting	Gain more input from others prior to meetings.
Special Initiative	6	3	Varies	30-60 min	Roll out special initiative to the whole organization (sometimes for smaller groups)	Invite all stakeholders.
Executive Briefing	5	1-2	2-10	60 min	Briefing to executives on training efforts and initiative; and results	Target-poll selected executives.
Budget Review	6	1	2-10	60 min	Annual opportunity to present to executive team about needed budget	Leverage interactive handouts.

For more on defining your presentation universe, see http://www.mrpresentation.com/presentation universe.

the job. Indeed, two different people can perform the same identical actions during the workday and experience them in opposite ways, just as two people can be involved in the same car accident but one will think he was unlucky for getting in the accident in the first place, whereas the other will think she is profoundly lucky to be alive. Presentation Masters tend to be optimists who are on the lookout for a positive outcome from any given situation; it's one of the mental habits they consciously develop as a means of creating their own "luck."

Masters may look like "lucky" people because a disproportionate number of things seem to go their way, but the truth isn't quite so mystical. Presentation Masters are very adept at organizing and orchestrating their time to accelerate the rate at which their goals and objectives are met, and this constant forward motion gives their working lives a sense of direction and purpose. They do this by having clear goals and objectives in the first place and by linking their thoughts and actions to those goals in a way that emphasizes action, efficiency, and results. The more results they get, the more confident they become, and the cycle of success starts feeding on itself, reinforcing the Master's effectiveness and accelerating success.

Two Presentation Types: Scheduled and Unscheduled

When thinking about this dynamic for the first time, it helps to divide presentations into two separate categories: scheduled presentations (those that involve some measure of formal preparation) and ad hoc, or impromptu, presentations (interactions that aren't planned, but require an element of persuasion or explanation). Most learning professionals give formal presentations quite regularly and often deliver the same basic material over and over again, so they are comfortable with scheduled presentations. Such presentations usually have clear expectations and well-defined content. This also holds true in the larger professional world, especially in sales or marketing, where formal presentations are part of the job. The area that most people struggle with—if they recognize the problem at all—is spontaneous presentations, the dozens of opportunities that arise every day to exert some sort of influence on those around us. One big blind spot people have is in thinking of formal presentations as having a beginning, middle, and end and, most important, *failing to recognize the connection between their success in planned presentations and the success or failure of their unplanned, spontaneous presentations.*

Learning and Strategy, Hand in Hand

A new breed of learning professionals finding themselves much more involved in executing the strategic vision of their organization and less involved in what they refer to as "traditional learning activities," as the example of Holly Huntley on the following page shows. The two go hand in hand now, so it's just as important to know how to make an airtight business case for training and make productive use of the coveted "seat at the table" as it is to be up to speed on the latest training techniques. For consultants, coaches, content providers, and other vendors working from the outside, marketing your services effectively means knowing more about client companies than ever before: what their strategies are, their tactics for achieving those strategies, who in the company is responsible for what, who the competition is, and so forth. Once hired, it also means knowing when and how to jump into the strategic flow of things and deliver relevant, effective solutions whose value proposition cannot be questioned.

You probably already know all that, but what you may not know is how to tackle these new challenges in your daily work life. What should you do differently? How, exactly, can you generate opportunities and capitalize on them to become one of those "lucky" successful dynamos? For instance, how do you go about generating consensus and ensuring buy-in? How do you make a persuasive business case for training? Once you have metrics, how do you make them tell a compelling story? How do you communicate the value of such intangibles as morale and loyalty? How do you manage the transition between an old-school, order-taking, transactional learning environment to a proactive, responsive environment that drives strategic change? These and other questions are covered in the coming chapters.

From Preparation to Excellence

Holly Huntley is the CLO for Computer Sciences Corporation, a global information systems company that employs 78,000 people worldwide. To secure consistent buy-in and support from the top of her organization, Huntley estimates that she spends the majority of her time on the job working behind the scenes to make sure everyone understands what her department is doing in the way of learning and performance, and why.

"A big part of what I do is sales and marketing," says Huntley. "I spend a lot of time building the business case for programs and developing value propositions. I have to identify all the stakeholders, understand their issues and concerns, and weigh those against others' competing concerns. I test ideas out in the field, measure cost data, talk to people, then draft a framework, and test it to make sure the value proposition is there."

Huntley only does a couple of formal presentations a year for her chief operating officer (COO) and the company's management team, but the success of those presentations hinges, she says, on the careful preparation she and her team put into the plan. "In my role, I do very little that's related to traditional learning skills. What I do is relationship building. I'm tapping into sales, marketing, management, organizational change—all to build an airtight business case for what we do." Huntley leaves nothing to chance, she says, and she makes sure she knows what everyone is thinking before she ever opens her mouth in front of her COO. "I have a call plan, and I spend days just going around and talking to people about their needs and how we can help them. It's one of the most important things I do, though, because it's essential for building buy-in and consensus."

Although she's never studied Presentation Mastery, Huntley is someone who operates according to similar principles because she has discovered, through trial and error, that managing the small things along the way helps make the big things fall into place. For example, if a message is important to get across, many people might think it sufficient to tell people once, twice, or maybe three times at the most to make sure they get it. Huntley and her team don't stop there. They have a saying—"seven times, seven ways"—to reinforce the idea that important messages must be repeated in person, over the phone, in email memos, on the company bulletin board, in the company newsletter seven times to make sure the message is driven home.

Huntley believes that making sure all of these background details are addressed is one of the most important keys to her success. "In a large, matrixed organization like CSC, it's very difficult to align with all the different stakeholders and understand what the rules of engagement are for all of our business units. They're all different, so navigating all that complexity is a huge challenge," she explains.

She does deliver formal presentations to management on occasion, but Huntley doesn't consider them the most important presentations of the year because, she says, "If I've done my job right, those presentations are just a formality. I would never walk into that room without knowing whom I can count on for support and where I can expect resistance and why."

We're not talking about how to squeeze more tasks into your day. We're talking about new ways of thinking and working that fit the diverse demands of the global marketplace; reflect important changes in the evolving theories of organizational change and behavior; take advantage of current communication technologies; and recognize the realities of how power, influence, motivation, and leadership are accumulated and deployed in a modern organization.

It's a complex subject, and it's no wonder so many people in the field of learning and performance feel so confused. The key to meeting these new job demands is the increasing importance of communication as a means of gathering information and as a means of exerting power and influence, as well as the importance of being prepared to communicate effectively anytime, anywhere; that is, Presentation Mastery.

The Next Level: Level 3

Ultimately, the reason Presentation Mastery is such a powerful, career-changing concept is that those who practice it well are making the most of their mind, personal network, influence, abilities, and resources. Unlike people who approach their job with a haphazard attitude toward the outcome of their daily interactions, Presentation Masters always have their goals in mind, are prepared to articulate their ideas, even on a moment's notice, and have the skill and confidence to exert a greater degree of influence on people whose support, trust, respect, and cooperation they rely upon. If there is any magic in the mix, it involves being mentally agile enough to see the opportunities available, then developing the instincts through discipline and practice to act on them quickly. Do this dozens of times a day and hundreds of times a week, and the benefits start to add up. Gradually, as you build power, respect, and self-confidence, you are able to get more of what you want and less of what you don't want. You are no longer fighting yourself, your organization, or both, and you are working in harmony to execute a specific strategy and achieve a series of clearly articulated goals. The result for those who operate consistently at level 3 of Presentation Mastery is that more decisions go their way, fewer obstacles impede their progress, and the layering of one positive interaction upon another snowballs into a successful, rewarding career.

In the following chapters, we will be explaining how to apply specific principles of Presentation Mastery to the emerging challenges faced by learning professionals everywhere, whether working from within an organization or assisting it from the outside. By reading this chapter, you have already taken the first step toward Mastery, which is recognizing how the principles of Mastery can help you achieve your goals as a learning professional. The next step is identifying opportunities to improve your own skills, after which you will develop strategies for improving the outcomes in your entire presentation universe.

Very Important Points

- Workplace learning professionals must develop new and more powerful ways of communicating and presenting themselves to colleagues and the organization.

- Informing, persuading, building consensus, ensuring buy-in, demonstrating value, selling, marketing, politicking—these are all skills workplace learning professionals must possess to thrive in the 21st century.

- Tony Jeary's concept of Presentation Mastery is one that learning professionals should embrace because it encompasses the communication skills learning professionals need to excel.

- Learning professionals should aspire to operate at level 3 of the Presentation Mastery curve where the dividends of superior communication pay off exponentially, both in one's professional and personal life.

- Understand that presentations aren't just formal, scheduled stand-and-deliver affairs. Almost all business communication—phone calls, email, video- and audioconferencing, meetings, lunches—involve an element of presentation.

- The definition of a presentation is "the act of working to change the content of another person's mind at a particular time and place." It's what learning professionals do every day, so you should aspire to do it to the best of your ability.

- Learn how to use the magic of Mastery, which comes in knowing how to say the right thing, at the right time, to the right people, in a way that ensures that one's short-term goals are met and the foundation for meeting long-term goals is laid.

- Define your presentation universe, that is, all the ways in which you deliver both formal and informal presentations. This is the first step toward operating at level III on the presentation impact curve. Take it, and your journey toward Mastery will begin.

Now that you know more about the Presentation Mastery approach, let's start moving along the presentation impact curve. The next chapter looks at some of the competencies you'll need to become a proactive Presentation Master and introduces a model for thinking about how to develop, articulate, and initiate learning in any organization.

The Proactive Learning Professional

To the Point

In the learning profession, being proactive is no longer a choice; it's an imperative. Since at least the 1970s, workplace learning and performance professionals have been trying to become more than just deliverers of courses and content; they've been working their way into positions of influence so that they can have a greater impact on the organizations they serve. Being a proactive learning professional means much more than simply picking up the phone before it rings; it means thinking about one's role in an organization in an entirely different way. It means approaching one's job strategically and having clear and aligned goals, high aspirations, and a deliberate plan of action. It also means working harder and smarter to achieve your own personal goals, which, in turn, will enhance your career as a learning professional.

Twenty-First Century Competencies

In 2004, ASTD developed its competency model for learning and performance, which is the foundation of the ASTD Certification Institute's professional certification program (figure 3-1). The purpose of the model is to illustrate the capabilities required of learning professionals to be successful in the expanding global economy. The model is divided into three separate levels. At the pyramid's base are foundational competencies, or general skills everyone should develop. In the middle of the pyramid are areas of expertise (AOEs), which include job functional areas such as designing learning, delivering training, measuring and evaluating, and so on. At the top of the pyramid are the various roles a learning professional might play depending on the needs of the organization at that time, such as learning strategist, business partner, project manager, or professional specialist.

Any single individual might play one or more of the roles at the top of the model, as well as be adept in multiple AOEs. But, for any of these efforts to be successful, the skills at the bottom of the pyramid—the foundational competencies—must be developed, nurtured, and, eventually, mastered. The reason these skills appear at the base of the competency model is that they are the foundation upon which everything else is built. Without them, or with only a few of them, the whole edifice begins to crumble. These foundational competencies are themselves divided into three different categories:

- *Interpersonal:* building trust, communicating effectively, influencing stakeholders, leveraging diversity, and networking and partnering
- *Business/management:* analyzing needs and proposing solutions, applying business acumen, driving results, planning and implementing assignments, and thinking strategically
- *Personal:* demonstrating adaptability and modeling personal development.

Figure 3-1. ASTD's Competency Model™ for workplace learning and performance.

The ASTD Competency Model™ serves as an excellent resource for professional growth and development for anyone in the workplace learning and performance field. Comprehensive enough to guide career development at all levels of the profession and covering a wider spectrum of roles than any previous ASTD model, it presents three layers of knowledge and skills: foundational competencies, areas of expertise, and workplace learning roles.

Source: Paul Bernthal et al., *ASTD Competency Study: Mapping the Future* (Alexandria, VA: ASTD Press, 2004.)

If you break these skills down, however, you'll find that all of the interpersonal competencies involve communication of some sort, and at least three of the business/management competencies (analyzing needs and proposing solutions, applying business acumen, and thinking strategically) require a frame of mind that often would be considered beyond the scope of the workplace learning profession. To be sure, ambitious learning professionals have always wanted to wield more influence with stakeholders and have yearned for a more significant strategic role in their organizations, but it's taken a long time to make top decision makers aware of the learning function's contribution.

Growing evidence suggests that executives everywhere are beginning to understand what learning professionals have known for so long: that properly trained learning professionals with a mandate for organizational excellence, unified support from the top, and the decision-making power to drive strategic change will directly contribute to the bottom line in ways that are measurable, repeatable, and sustainable. They can also make an organization more competitive, more desirable to work for, and turn it into a magnet for great talent. In some cases, they can even transform an entire organization and help lead the way for others to follow.

More Work, Bigger Payoffs

When we, the authors, talk about being proactive, the kinds of things David Vance (see sidebar on next page) does are what we are talking about. Vance did not simply provide reports that would satisfy his superiors; he went beyond to gather information that was very meaningful to them. In so doing, he also solidified his credibility as a leader and manager, earned the respect of his superiors and colleagues, established Caterpillar University as a valuable contributor to the organization's success, and likely secured for himself and his colleagues a much more budget-resilient future. Had he simply been a reactive manager, putting into place an adequate program that delivered acceptable results, his future might not be quite so bright.

Learning professionals who want to secure a brighter future for themselves need to think more like David Vance. They must be best-practice professionals who model the sort of strategic, forward-focused mindset that learning professionals at all levels need to cultivate *even if their organizations don't specifically ask them to.* In essence, a proactive

Caterpillar University

In the late 1990s, David Vance was Caterpillar Corporation's chief economist, but in 2001 he was hired to create what has since become one of the great success stories in corporate education: Caterpillar University. At the time, Caterpillar was feeling the growing pains that afflict most international companies at some point. With offices in Europe, Asia, and the Middle East, 92,000 employees, and dealers in 200 countries, Caterpillar—the world's leading manufacturer of construction and mining equipment, diesel and natural gas engines, and industrial gas turbines—had become a truly global entity. One of the biggest challenges global corporations face, of course, is maintaining and building upon the values that contributed to the organization's success in the first place. In 2001 Caterpillar became the first company to globally deploy Six Sigma, an increasingly popular discipline for measuring, evaluating, and eliminating errors and waste in various corporate processes. Along with that rollout, the company wanted a way to reach its people around the globe to reinforce company values in other important areas, such as leadership, career development, and change management. Caterpillar University was born to meet that need.

"The timing for Caterpillar U was good," recalls Vance. "Back then, most training was decentralized in the different business units, so it made sense to do something that focused on global learning needs." Exactly how that was going to happen, he wasn't sure, but he had ambitious goals for the entity he was creating, and knew how he wanted to position it strategically in the organization.

"I wanted to bring leadership to the learning function, so we began by focusing on opportunities that would make the greatest difference," Vance explains. Strategically speaking, one of the stated goals of Caterpillar U was to identify common global learning needs that would benefit the most number of employees. "As it happened, leadership training was one of the issues that was identified across the board as a need. Lots of people were moving around and interacting with lots of different groups around the country and world, so it made sense to develop a common language and approach for leadership—a standard model—for everyone."

The pilot program developed from this effort, "Making Great Leaders," was so successful that it has since been cascaded to all 7,000 of Caterpillar's management leaders. By 2005, Caterpillar University had developed six different colleges—leadership, marketing and distribution, technology, business and business processes, six sigma, and product support—and was gearing up to meet the additional learning needs for all 28 of the company's business units.

Building Caterpillar University's credibility within the company was not a slam-dunk, however. According to Vance, there were skeptics in the ranks, and the overall cost of the venture was high on the list of concerns. Although the University had the green light from upper management, containing costs and delivering measurable results were priorities from the start. Fortunately, Vance's background as an economist made him not only comfortable with numbers, but also aware of how important those numbers could be to the eventual success of Caterpillar U.

"I like numbers and data, and they were something I wanted from the very start," says Vance. "I wanted to make sure we were really getting value from our learning. What are the costs and benefits? How much value does this program have? I want to know. I never know anything for sure, but putting a number on something helps clarify things. I encourage people to think through every aspect of a program. If the value is intangible, I ask people to estimate it. If they think a program is going to improve safety, I ask them to tell me why."

When developing the metrics by which the University's success would ultimately be judged, however, Vance did not simply provide the data that upper management wanted to see; he began tracking the program's success in what he calls "stealth mode."

"Containing costs was upper management's first priority, but after that they would have been satisfied with rather basic level 1 feedback: Would employees recommend a course to others? Can they apply it to their job? Is it relevant to their work? But, we wanted to go much deeper, so we began doing our own measurements, which we didn't start sharing until we got some confidence in the numbers. This deeper feedback went all the way to level 5 in some cases, and the results we uncovered were nothing short of amazing. It took a few years, but I can now say with absolute confidence, and with data to back me up, that Caterpillar University returns a net benefit to the company of $100 million and that the ROI is in the neighborhood of 200 percent." Vance laughs when he says this, because he knows those numbers are close to being unbelievable. He also knows that if he hadn't patiently collected the data to support this claim and hadn't revealed the results of his investigations gradually to upper management, no one would have believed him in the company, either.

"If I had told my CEO on the first day that I was going to give him a 200 percent ROI, he would have thought I was crazy," says Vance. The key to his success, he says, was going slowly, collecting as much data as possible (but not sharing it all), patiently building the business case so that he could tell the story behind the numbers, and being humble about the results.

"Among other things, it was important that we build our credibility within the company," explains Vance. "We've got lots of engineers and analytical types, and they want numbers. Being able to give them what they want helps build credibility. If you keep track of what works and what doesn't work, can show measurable results over time, and can show that you have projections and estimates for everything, including intangibles, then people will respect you. They'll know that you're running it [the learning function] like a business."

learning professional is one who has acquired all of the traditional skills associated with learning in terms of course design, project management, and delivery, but also recognizes the realities of the 21st-century workplace and is dedicated to developing and perfecting the skills necessary to function effectively in this new, demanding, business environment.

This new role is strategic in more than one sense. Yes, it means aligning one's activities more directly with the organization's stated business strategies, but it also means viewing one's role in a different light. If you are working on the inside, it means seeing yourself less as an employee than as an internal "consultant" who happens to have an office in the building. If you're an outside consultant, coach, or vendor, it means thinking of yourself less as a purveyor of learning solutions than as an extension of the organization's learning department, one that is expected to understand as much about the organization's strategies, goals, and tactics as those working inside the company. It also means consciously positioning oneself as a person whose knowledge and insight add value and whose efforts are perceived by others to always be in the best interests of the organization. It ultimately means thinking and acting as if the fate of the organization is on your shoulders. Yes, this transformation does mean more work, but it's work that will pay back dividends a hundred times over.

The SPEAK Model

To get you moving in the right direction, we've developed a five-part mnemonic model for thinking about how to develop, articulate, and link learning in any organization. Its purpose is to provide you with an easy-to-remember, general foundation of principles upon which to base your enhanced role in the organization. We will be exploring aspects of the model throughout the book, but we call it the SPEAK model (figure 3-2) because communication is at its core:

- **S**trategy
- **P**reparation, **P**ractice, **P**ersonalization
- **E**xecution
- **A**ccountability
- **K**nowledge.

The SPEAK model is really a life cycle in which each part informs every other part, which, when combined, provide a replicable process for exceptional learning contributions. Let's take a look at each component of the model.

Figure 3-2. The SPEAK model.

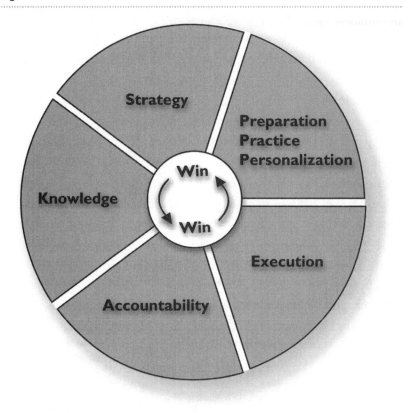

S = Strategy

A 2004 study commissioned by Convergys and conducted by Saratoga/PricewaterhouseCoopers revealed that the majority of executives polled at more than 300 companies worldwide cited "misalignment of business and workforce strategies" as a major obstacle to revenue improvement (Saratoga/PWC and Beatty, 2005). Eighty-four percent of large global companies said they were not using their workforce to its full potential. Only 16 percent rated their company as being agile enough to reallocate human resources based on strategic need. And, more than half of the U.S. executives polled admitted that their organizations were not proficient at training and developing their top talent.

To align workforce strategies with your senior leadership's overarching organizational goals, you have to know what your CEO and other executives view as the main challenges facing their businesses today. The findings of the Conference Board's CEO Challenge 2006 survey, summarized in table 3-1, revealed what's on CEOs' minds (Rudis, 2006).

The fact is, many organizations do not clearly articulate their strategies and objectives, even to their own employees. The reason: aligning these strategies is easier said than done. The consequence: alignment suffers and an organization's strategic objectives aren't achieved as quickly or as well as they should be. That's why learning professionals who want to play an active business role need to develop a deep understanding of organizational strategy and help link that knowledge with the practical means for attaining it.

Table 3-1. Top challenges and priorities identified by CEOs.

Ranking	Challenge or Priority	Percentage of CEOs Identifying as "of Greatest Concern"
1	Sustained and steady top-line growth	37.5%
2	Profit growth	36.1
3	Consistent execution of strategy by top management	33.4
4	Speed, flexibility, adaptability to change	33.1
5	Customer loyalty and retention	29.4
6	Stimulating innovation and creativity; enabling entrepreneurship	23.9
7	Corporate reputation	22.9
8	Speed to market	22.7
9	[Product] innovation	20.8
10	Improving productivity	20.3

Source: Rudis, E. (2006). *CEO Challenge 2006: Perspectives and Analysis.* New York: The Conference Board.

If you want to serve an organization better, you must know precisely what its strategic objectives are and devote yourself to finding ways to achieve them. Your commitment must be equal to or greater than that of the CEO because the CEO only demands results; you are responsible for delivering them.

P = Preparation, Practice, Personalization

The *P* of the SPEAK model refers to preparation, practice, and personalization. For Presentation Masters, preparation is really a lifelong process of information gathering and relationship building, combined with a dedication to excellence that shows in every detail. Even when they don't have a formal presentation for which to prepare, Masters are always gathering stories and anecdotes that might sharpen their message; reading books and magazines to keep current in their industry; organizing websites and articles for future use; and generally being a sponge for any kind of information that can help them communicate to their audiences.

In formal presentations, extensive preparation is the key to calming nerves and achieving peak performance. Presentation Masters go over every detail of a presentation and leave nothing to chance. They research their audience thoroughly, tailor their message accordingly, do their best to anticipate any question or issue that might crop up, and have answers ready, just in case.

Masters embrace a daily regimen of disciplines to help them hone their communication skills. They continually practice their craft, paying conscious attention to how they use all types of communication, including telephone conversations, email, meetings, seminars, web conferencing, and videoconferencing. All offer opportunities to practice various aspects of the art of communication. Masters don't squander these opportunities; they capitalize on them and learn as much as they can from each exchange.

Personalization is a critical aspect of Presentation Mastery because communication happens between people, not between departments and organizations. In almost every case, the more personal communication is, the better. It is better to say thank you in person, for instance, than to say it in an email. It is better to talk to people one-on-one than it is to talk to them in a group. Listening, eye contact, a firm handshake, conversational skills, knowledge of an audience—these are all important because they help reinforce the personal nature of communication. Much of professional life is about working with, for, or through other people, so knowing how to build strong personal relationships is central to success. Masters know this, so they try to personalize their communication as much as possible.

E = Execution

Whenever Tiger Woods enters a golf tournament, people expect him to win every time because he is the most strategically astute golfer in the world, and his devotion to preparation and practice is legendary. But even Tiger does not win every time, because, as he himself says, "...Just because I feel comfortable about my game doesn't guarantee I'm going to play well. I still have to execute" (Both, 2003). Superior strategy and preparation are useless without great execution. Execution is doing what needs to be done and using all of the knowledge and experience you've collected over the years to do it as well as you can.

When presenting learning, however, execution also means having all of the little things that you've done over the weeks and months add up to a successful outcome. It means paying attention to detail, devoting yourself to excellence and working hard every day to do the best job you can. To operate at a high level of mastery, one's habits and energies must be devoted to aligning many small but important details that will eventually add up to a big win. Execution is quality in action. Without it, everything else tends to fall apart.

A = Accountability

For too long, the field of learning and human performance has been thought of by many as a "soft" discipline that often operates outside of typical business parameters and does not embrace the idea of accountability using business metrics. That perception has to change, for three reasons:

- To function efficiently, organizations need to know the learning function's true impact on the enterprise in common business terms.

- The health of workplace learning as a profession depends upon the learning professional's ability to accurately monitor and articulate learning's contribution to organizations, in the only language CEOs understand—the language of business.

- Rigorous, business-oriented management of learning is the only way to gain the long-term respect and cooperation of decision makers.

In the personal sense, accountability is basically doing what you say you're going to do. In the professional world, it's not enough just to take someone's word for it; there must be some objective criteria for evaluating people's performance. In learning, that means finding ways to measure the effect of learning on employees, as well as its overall contribution to the enterprise. Performance expectations are the benchmarks against which everything in an organization is measured, and learning is no different. Senior management typically measures performance by a number of key metrics and indicators, particularly financial ones. Part of your job is to understand those metrics and, insofar as possible, package results—the ultimate value to the enterprise—in the form these metrics require.

Therefore, an important part of the proactive learning professional's job is to help develop effective and accurate measurement tools and to insist on having metrics that accurately track and report learning's value to the enterprise. Being accountable to the organization in this way is an important step in the quest for business respectability. Consequently, making sure that learning is just as accountable to upper management as any other department is primary. Only by making learning's value known on the balance sheet will that seat at the table ever start to feel comfortable.

K = Knowledge

It comes as no surprise that in the knowledge economy, knowledge itself is the currency of the realm. Learning professionals are chiefly responsible for two types of knowledge: individual knowledge, including their own, and institutional knowledge, or the collective knowledge of an enterprise. Most training is geared toward teaching individuals what they need to know to do their jobs. The trickier part of the puzzle—and the one that learning professionals must become more adept at—is managing the complex network of human relationships that exists in every organization.

Learning how an organization learns, that is, how the organization processes information to achieve the most competitive, profitable outcome possible, is becoming an important part of the learning professional's job. It's no longer enough to develop great content that meets an organization's surface needs; the learning professional must also be deeply aware of how an organization functions at an organic level in terms of its people, culture, attitudes, politics, and so forth. Then, the professional must translate that knowledge into effective learning solutions.

The Proactive Ideal

The proactive workplace learning professional knows how to leverage training so that it has a measurable strategic impact on an organization whether he or she is working on the inside of an organization or helping it from the outside. Most organizations are moving toward a blended model that uses both internal and external channels by handling some of their training inside and outsourcing other training functions. The trend is toward smaller internal departments with more discretion about when and where to spend money on outside resources, so knowing both sides of the fence can also be a strategic asset. Therefore, it pays to know how to be proactive whether you are working as an internal or external workplace learning professional.

Before setting out on a journey, however, it helps to know what the destination is. Proactive learning professionals do their jobs differently from reactive ones, and proactive learning departments function differently from reactive ones. The differences are profound. However, the truth is that few learning functions in the working world are either 100 percent proactive or 100 percent reactive. Most use a mixture of both approaches, depending on the circumstances if only because there are some aspects of training (employee orientation, routine maintenance tasks, compliance-based training, and so forth) that don't require regular reinvention. Organizations making the transition from reactive to proactive often outsource routine training functions and maintain smaller internal departments that have a strategic planning role. Indeed, fully proactive learning departments tend to be "channel agnostic." Their focus is on providing efficient and effective solutions, and they will choose the options that are best for the organization, whether it involves buying, building, hiring, or creating them.

Characteristics of Proactive Learning

Ultimately, it's a competitive advantage for companies to be as proactive as possible. Table 3-2 presents a list of characteristics that are typical of workplace learning in a proactive mode. Most of these characteristics also apply to individuals as well, and in the final analysis the two cannot be separated. So take a moment to go down the list and check off the ones that are true about you or your department.

Very Important Points

- Study the ASTD Competency Model for Workplace Learning and Performance. It is an important blueprint for the types of skills and roles that 21st-century learning professionals will be required to master.
- Insofar as possible, model your career aspirations and behavior after best-practice professionals who are already paving the way.
- Memorize the SPEAK model of learning effectiveness (S = Strategy; P = Preparation, Practice, Personalization; E = Execution; A = Accountability; and K = Knowledge).

Table 3-2. Characteristics of the proactive workplace learning professional and learning function.

Please work your way down the checklist to identify which characteristics you and your department possess.

Characteristic	You ✓	Your Learning Department ✓
1. Acts as a strategic partner in running the organization		
2. Understands the organization's strategic objectives, and exists to support them		
3. Has secured support from top executives, particularly the CEO		
4. Has solid business reasons for everything it does and can make the case for it anytime, anywhere		
5. Meets regularly with upper management to make sure goals and strategies are aligned		
6. Systems are in place to hire, train, develop, nurture, reward, and retain high performers		
7. Actively seeks to identify skills gaps, hot spots, ticking time bombs, and other potential problem areas		
8. Leverages organization's strengths for maximum advantage and impact		
9. Proposes solutions for addressing both current and future strategic imperatives		
10. Regularly offers creative alternatives to existing programs and methods		
11. Doesn't waste time on nice-to-haves; focuses on core needs and solutions		
12. Uses Presentation Mastery, balanced scorecard, or a similar system to align organizational strategy, learning, performance, and results		
13. Continually tracks its own performance and seeks ways to improve		

Characteristic	You ✓	Your Learning Department ✓
14. Activities directly impact the bottom line in a measurable way		
15. Learning results and organizational strategy are linked by appropriate metrics		
16. All outcomes, even intangible ones, are measured in some way		
17. Current methodologies are constantly being compared to industry best practices and updated as necessary		
18. Studies the latest technologies, and uses them when appropriate		
19. Continually reviews its own performance and learns from mistakes		
20. Always looking for, and finding, ways to improve performance		
21. Actively meets with and seeks input from a wide variety of stakeholders		
22. Team members are energetic and work with a sense of urgent purpose		
23. Significantly impacts the organization's ability to meets its strategic goals/objectives		
24. Consistently attracts the best and brightest talent in the field		
25. Provides advice to help leaders make quality decisions		
26. Involves organizational leaders in deployment and execution of programs		
27. Isn't afraid to outsource when it makes sense for the organization to do so		
28. Is admired and respected both inside the organization and out		

(continued on next page)

Table 3-2. Characteristics of the proactive workplace learning professional and learning function (continued).

Characteristic	You ✓	Your Learning Department ✓
29. Results are consistent, reliable, and repeatable		
30. Responds quickly to organizational needs		
31. Has multiple solutions for problems and isn't stuck in a program rut		
32. Seeks out and welcomes outside evaluation, input, and advice		
33. Is perceived in the organization as a driver of performance and leadership		
34. Finds ways to use training as a problem solver in untraditional ways		
35. Is fully aware of intradepartmental conflicts and other turf issues and seeks diplomatic solutions		
36. Is perceived within the organization as an agent of change		
37. Understands and can articulate the organization's entire value chain		
38. Knows where value is created, where it is not, and where opportunities are being overlooked		
39. Knows which metrics matter most in the organization		
40. Doesn't push its own agenda and builds consensus wherever possible		

When you're done, count the number of checkmarks for you and your learning function. There are 40 total, so if you or your organization scored more than 20, you are well on your way to working proactively in the learning profession. Items you didn't check are areas to keep in mind as you read the rest of this book because that's where you will likely need to focus when it comes time to take specific actions.

■ Remember, it's called the SPEAK model because communication is the crucial core competency that connects all its components.

■ Use table 3-2 to determine which characteristics of proactive learning you already practice—and which ones you don't.

Now, in chapter 4, let's take a closer look at the nuts and bolts of effective communication that you can apply in every presentation, whether it's a five-minute phone call or a two-day team-building program.

The Strategic Power
of Communication

To the Point

D ecision makers want to see a meaningful relationship between learning initiatives and results, which, because of the interdependent nature of learning, can be difficult to provide. Many learning professionals expend a tremendous amount of energy trying to generate concrete ROI numbers, without recognizing that it's equally important to make a persuasive case for learning's overall strategic impact on an organization. Communication is the means by which learning spreads throughout an organization, so one of the best ways learning can align itself is by heightening awareness of the strategic importance of communication and facilitating more precise and purposeful communication throughout the organization. The great side benefit of this approach: Learning's contribution and value will be difficult, if not impossible, to dispute.

Alignment = Value + Communication

What decision makers really want to see is a direct cause-and-effect relationship between learning initiatives and results, period. But, as every learning professional knows, such relationships are often difficult to establish because there are so many extraneous and intangible factors involved. It is also difficult to isolate a specific learning solution as *the* cause for a particular success. But, business-minded people hate guessing. They want proof.

Alignment is the word most often used to describe the existence of direct causal links between an organization's objectives, the actions it takes to achieve those objectives, and the process by which the results of those actions are measured. It may sound simple in concept, but achieving alignment can be quite challenging and complicated in practice, and part of the problem lies in the areas of presentation and communication, which are our focus here.

One Person's Communication Is Another Person's...

Unfortunately, many official statements of mission and strategy sound like empty business jargon. What does it really mean when a company's mission is to "develop task-specific, scalable enterprise solutions that leverage optimal operational synergies and facilitate transparent workplace modalities to effectively meet or exceed stakeholder expectations"? And, how on earth would one link a strategy to such a mission statement?

Indeed, communicating strategies and objectives in a way that everyone can understand is a challenge for many organizations. A CEO may issue a demand for "organic growth," or "more efficient deployment of resources," which might sound good and leader-like on paper, but to rank-and-file employees, it may mean nothing more than just another call to do more with less. If strategic objectives are communicated in vague, hollow language, even if the verbiage has been approved by the organization's leaders, it can take some work to sift through the verbal fog to locate a true strategy and the consequences that arise from it.

Bland or imprecise language does not render a statement unimportant. A strategy might be as innocuous-sounding as "Star Corporation will explore new international market opportunities," but it makes an enormous amount of difference whether that "international" strategy is being undertaken because the company has exhausted its growth potential in the United States or if it is being implemented because international appetites for the company's products are so voracious that the company has to expand to keep up with demand. Those are two entirely different business scenarios. Because the context is different in each, execution of that strategy will require entirely different responses from the people inside those respective organizations. In fact, depending on the company, that same dull but important sentence could apply to hundreds of different business plans.

To complicate matters, most organizations pursue multiple strategies simultaneously, so it's important to know how the pieces fit together. At construction- and farm-equipment builder Caterpillar, for instance, executives and managers are required to memorize the company's core values and strategies. At such high-performing organizations, alignment between learning and corporate strategy is usually a high priority and, at companies such as IBM, is even a stated strategy itself. IBM's ability to stay competitive is linked directly to its ability to learn and translate this knowledge into business results. The company's learning paradigm can be summed up quite succinctly: "The perception of the learning function is shifting from being an operating cost to becoming a strategic lever that can add value at multiple levels of the organization. Learning's focus is moving from training and certification to all facets of learning including collaboration, knowledge management, analytics, and performance improvement. Once pushed at workers in their silos, learning now pulls in everyone in the firm's value chain" (IBM Global Services, 2005).

Why Communication Is a Strategic Asset

Now, if you ask someone whether good communication is an important part of the strategic value chain, the response probably will be yes because that's what everyone thinks. The irony is that often communication isn't something people think about much at all. Relatively few people understand how truly important communication effectiveness is for organizational health, and fewer still treat communication skills as a strategic asset.

In a sense, communication is the glue that holds an enterprise's value chain together. Within organizations, presentations are the primary form of communication for delivering and executing strategic objectives. But, presentations across an organization are not confined to formal, stand-and-deliver presentations in a conference room. In reality, presentations occur all the time, in both informal and formal settings, and enormous amounts of information are exchanged. Table 4-1 offers some examples of presentations that typically happen in organizations and describes some possible roles for the workplace learning function.

Based on the list in table 4-1, if you added up the number of presentations your organization engages in on any given day, how many would it be in a day? In a week? In a month? As you can see, it's easily possible to have hundreds or even thousands of presentations going on in an organization daily. Each of these interactions involves an information exchange of some sort, and each of these exchanges has some relevance to the overall business of the organization.

Once you appreciate the volume of communications occurring in any given organization, it's easier to understand how various inaccuracies, misunderstandings, and points of confusion can multiply into larger problems. This multiplier effect is the great communication killer in many large organizations. Unfortunately, most organizations plagued by this problem aren't even aware of it; they just take it for granted that good ideas don't necessarily go anywhere; that action items aren't necessarily followed up on; that a certain level of confusion or noise in communication channels is normal; that redundant messages are unavoidable; and that conflicting messages from the top are bound to happen. None of these things is inevitable, though. They are only certain to happen if the organization doesn't do anything to prevent them.

Table 4-1. Typical types of presentations occurring in organizations.

Presentation Type	Role of Workplace Learning Function
Meetings	Leadership, time management, presentation skills
Sales calls	Sales training, product knowledge
Training sessions	Program/content development and delivery
Facilitated events	Programming/delivery
Speeches	Executive coaching, general presentation skills
Seminars	Content development/delivery
One-on-one sessions	Management skills, leadership development, coaching
Electronic presentations (e.g., videoconferences, web conferences, online collaborations, email)	Technical competence, online presentation skills
Telephone and audioconferences	Presentation skills, advance materials production, technical competence
Print (newsletters, memos, hand-outs, annual reports, and so forth)	Materials production, message consistency
Branding, advertising, and merchandising	Message consistency
Marketing and public relations	Message consistency, general management skills
Customer interactions (for example, support services)	Call-center training, technical support training, customer service training
Media opportunities (radio, television, journalist interviews, webinars, and so on)	Media literacy, presentation skills, executive coaching

In most organizations, learning professionals are not responsible for shaping core messages; that responsibility typically falls to the CEO and the senior management team, along with such departments as communications, marketing, public relations, and HR. Learning professionals at any level can ensure that the messages they receive and pass along are clear and consistent with the strategy with which they are associated.

They can also encourage colleagues to reframe their thinking about the presentation or communication component of management by, for example, showing what happens when communications are muddled and unfocused. In the world of workplace learning, this often happens when a program is mandated, but employees see little or no connection between the content of the program and their job, much less a connection between the program and an organization's larger strategic objectives. Such disconnects can breed low morale, cynicism, and sometimes contempt for management. Even worse, it only takes one or two off-message training experiences for employees to conclude that *all* training is irrelevant, and that *all* messages issued from the corporate suites can be safely ignored.

The Meeting Diet

Time is another factor that few people consider in the overall communication puzzle. Consider meetings. How often do you find yourself in meetings that run long? Meetings that should have ended but drag on because the room is reserved for another 20 minutes? Meetings during which material from previous meetings is repeated? This loose attitude about people's time wastes countless hours of productivity every year. Simply instituting a set of procedures for meetings that everyone is required to adhere to can save an enormous amount of time; it can also benefit an organization by boosting morale and energizing the troops. The ground rules can be as simple as deciding when to end a meeting and sticking to it. At the deeper levels of Presentation Mastery, however, meeting ground rules might involve:

- setting a clear agenda
- assigning homework, or prework, to be completed ahead of time
- writing down specific goals for every meeting
- making sure the right people are present at any given meeting, including the decision makers, to ensure that things move along

- meeting for specific purposes only
- not meeting if you don't have to
- only meeting for as long as is necessary to accomplish specific goals
- conducting a meeting with central goals in mind at all times
- keeping digressions and meandering to a minimum
- assigning a timekeeper or moderator to keep things on track
- closing the meeting with clear summaries and action plans
- implementing a consistent set of follow-up procedures to make sure good ideas and necessary action items don't dissolve into the mist
- standardizing meeting procedures across the organization
- creating a standard meeting template for everyone to use
- adhering strictly to meeting times
- creating an enterprisewide set of meeting rules and procedures
- making sure everyone in the organization understands the strategic importance of adhering to the rules
- ensuring that a skilled facilitator is either managing or assisting the meeting.

Most people will read the preceding list and say to themselves, "Yes, these are things we probably should be doing, but aren't." The difference between an average organization and one that is operating as if communications are an important *strategic imperative* is that its people actually *do* the things most others only talk about. They link strategies and programs; they make sure their communications are consistent; they set goals and achieve them; they manage their time with discipline and respect for others; they have a purpose and plan for everything, and they do not deviate from it. What happens in such organizations is that taking care of all of those little details ends up paying huge dividends over time. In terms of messaging and communication, information flows through the pipe cleanly when confusion is minimal and people don't have to double-check information, or worse, act on incorrect information, discover their mistakes, back-track, and start over. Messages that cascade seamlessly through an organization make everyone's job easier and end up giving people more time and energy to devote to more important things—such as running the business.

Similar time-saving, alignment-focused procedures can be instituted for other types of interaction on the list as well. The average worker spends more than 90 minutes a day answering email, for instance. Think of the productivity gains if, through a few simple procedures, that average could be cut to a mere 60 minutes a day. In a company of 1,000 people, that's 500 hours saved every day or more than 125,000 hours of worker time every year!

A learning professional with a strategic mindset would hear that and think, "What if I could put together a one-hour seminar on email management, one that taught people a few simple, time-saving procedures?" Such a program would likely pay for itself in a single day and

Greater Efficiency at Firestone

Michael Gorey is president of Firestone Building Products Company, a subsidiary of Bridgestone Firestone dedicated to the commercial roofing industry. Gorey implemented many of the suggestions listed above for streamlining meetings because he was under tremendous pressure to expand the organization and make it more efficient.

"We are creating a bigger, more complicated business. We can't afford to have meetings that meander," says Gorey. "We can't afford to repeat things, have meetings that don't have conclusions or action items, or just meet for the sake of meeting. We're determined to have meetings that are as effective and efficient as possible because it serves our business goals to operate that way."

Gorey's company has doubled its revenue in the past three years, and he credits such efforts at organizational efficiency and focus as playing a large role in making that success possible.

reap dividends far into the future. Again, it's a simple idea—one many people might think of—but one that few organizations embrace with any sort of strategic urgency.

Learning Means Managing the Flow of Information

You may be wondering why we are focusing so much on the importance of alignment in *all* of an organization's communications when this particular book is about presenting learning. It's because effective communications are a core element of organizational success in the 21st century, and training plays a large part in the overall communication practices of any organization. If you think about it, learning professionals deal primarily with the flow of information through people, through technology, and through the organization. The information they manage affects the capabilities and competitiveness of the organization, as well as the quality of the leadership, the strength of the

Unifying Learning Functions

In August 2006, the Allianz Group, a global insurance corporation ranked 16th on the *Fortune* Global 500 list for 2006, hired Jeff Reeves, a former HR Vice President at Wal-Mart and PepsiCo, to run its training, HR, and communications functions, including corporate branding, and government relations, *all* out of one department. Reeves says he was hired "because I'm a businessperson first, an HR person second, and I have experience working in cross-functional teams." The decision to consolidate all of these disparate functions under him was a strategic one, he says, because these functions must work together anyway, and breaking down the reporting walls was a way to accomplish that objective and fuel Allianz's ambitious growth goals. Reeves intends to completely restructure Allianz's HR, training, and communications functions so that they operate on the "business partner" model, enabling them to respond more nimbly to the needs of the company and to be more accountable for everything they do.

culture, and the ultimate sustainability of the enterprise. Nothing could be more central, which is why many high-performing organizations choose to consolidate their training, HR, and communications functions into a single department or sometimes in one individual.

Seeking Ways to Add Value

For learning professionals to deliver the sort of value forward-thinking organizations are seeking, it's essential that they commit to a deep, organic understanding of their employer or client. Having worked hard to gain that deep understanding through independent study of publicly available material, conversations with co-workers and colleagues, purposeful interviews, and day-to-day experience, it should come as a relief to know this knowledge has a tremendous amount of practical value. It's particularly helpful in understanding an organization's business strategies and seeing how the energy flows through the enterprise via its core drivers. A careful analysis of how certain information travels through the value chain can open up all kinds of opportunities for learning to make a contribution. Such an analysis can also help cement learning's strategic role in an organization, particularly in places where it hasn't been regarded that way in the past.

Finding opportunities for you or your department to support or enhance an organizational strategy isn't always easy, and implementing them isn't always a cakewalk, either. New ideas are often met with resistance, so a certain amount of persuasion may be required to sell fixes of even the most obvious sort. It's worth the effort, however, and if you do it right, there can even be a measure of job security.

Essentially, what you're looking for when analyzing organizational strategy is ways to help the CEO and the rest of the management team achieve their goals, ways learning can be used to leverage the strengths and shore up the weaknesses of the organization, and ways learning can add value to the overall enterprise. Adding value is the key to maintaining a focused, business mindset. In essence, your one true responsibility to the organization for which you work, or with which you are consulting, is to make sure that the people and processes you manage are aligned with, and supportive of, the organization's strategies and objectives. Everything else is fluff.

Unfortunately, the training profession has been accused on more than one occasion of introducing far too much fluff into organizations. Regrettably, this may be true in some cases, but we're willing to bet that much of the time when programs are perceived as useless or irrelevant, it's not because the program itself is bad; it's because the learning practitioner responsible for the program failed to convince both superiors and learners of the program's practical value in terms of its contribution to the organization's stated mission, strategies, and objectives. In other words, the program failed because it wasn't presented correctly.

In many cases, it's not even the programs themselves that need to change, it's the thought processes behind them. So, once you've identified your organization's core strategies and objectives, here are a few of the questions you should ask yourself, if not senior management directly, about any given strategy:

- What needs to happen to make it a reality?
- What are the barriers to carrying out the strategy?
- How can the learning function help overcome the barriers?
- What are key measures or deliverables for this strategy?
- Who in the company is responsible for executing the strategy?
- Does the organization have the right skills/capabilities to deliver?
- Will there be any leadership transitions involved?
- Are the right people in the right places and do they have the right skill sets?
- Will processes need to be changed or overhauled?
- Is new technology involved? If so, will it require training?
- What are the organization's strengths and weaknesses?
- Are there ways to leverage the strengths to improve learning?

- Are there ways to shore up the weaknesses through learning?
- Looking ahead, do any what-if scenarios come to mind?
- What would happen if the workplace learning function did nothing?

Based on the answers to the foregoing questions, you may find strategic opportunities for workplace learning in such areas as the following:

- skills gaps
- leadership and management training
- speed-to-market issues
- other gaps related to limited organizational flexibility or agility
- mentoring/succession
- global expansion
- mergers and acquisitions
- underperforming departments or people
- entrenched, inefficient processes or operations
- new department and business initiatives
- business transformation
- goal acceleration initiatives
- risk/reward situations
- realignment of programs that do not sync with the strategy
- communication and presentation skills
- time management/productivity/efficiency
- knowledge management
- technical issues (hardware/software upgrades)
- morale issues
- innovations or new product development.

As always, the objective is to identify ways in which the learning function can support the organization's strategic vision. It's not always possible to identify opportunities instantaneously, however. Sometimes it takes time and patience to wait for opportunities to present themselves. Such situations call for "active waiting," according to Donald Sull, an associate professor of management practice at the London Business School (Sull, 2005). Active waiting means accepting the fact that nothing directly can be done in the present while remaining alert to opportunities and possibilities that may open up down the road and preparing to take advantage of new opportunities when they arise. Active waiting has some similarities to what Tony Jeary calls "always on" thinking, which means being plugged in and ready to act on a moment's notice, whenever that moment may happen. That's the kind of mindset one must maintain to be a true strategic partner, whether you're working inside an organization or consulting from the outside.

Case Study: Johnson Controls

Plug Yourself Into the Organizational Conversation

Every organization has a history, a catalog of stories that defines it, and every employee, consultant, and customer who interacts with that organization participates in the telling of that story in some way. To communicate effectively, learning professionals need to know the story of their organization, from the institutional knowledge that built it to the water-cooler conversation of business life that over weeks, months, and years shapes the texture and character of an organization.

In 2001, Janice Simmons took over as director of learning and development in the building management sector of Johnson Controls Incorporated (JCI) in Milwaukee, Wisconsin, a global company with 123,000 employees supported by more than 500 learning and development professionals. When Simmons arrived, JCI had just acquired York International, so integrating thousands of new employees was also part of the challenge.

Simmons says it took her at least three or four months to understand the situation she was facing. "My position had never existed before, because each department reported to different parts of the company. There had never been an organized, centralized learning function before, and no one really kept track of how much was being spent or whether the training supported the company's strategic plans. Back then, managers were used to picking up the phone telling the training department what they needed."

Still, Simmons was hired because her boss, the vice president of HR, believed the company wasn't getting as much value as it could out of its training operations. "They supported learning," Simmons says, "but the issue was how we, in learning and development, were supporting the company."

Simmons spent many months observing the company's trainers in action, talking with managers in various departments, and discussing learning issues with everyone in the company who reported directly to the president. When Simmons finally felt she understood what challenges the company faced, what its strategies and priorities were, and what her recommendations should be, she went to her boss and laid out her plan to turn JCI's learning and performance departments into a strategic business partner, or as she calls it, an "internal consulting firm."

"At the time, training at JCI was entirely reactive: they just did what they were told. I said to my boss, '*We* should be coming to *you* with ideas,' and he just looked at me and said, 'You're kidding.' He was floored. It had never occurred to anyone there to operate things that way."

Simmons' background is in consulting, so operating the learning and development functions as an in-house consulting department came naturally. Now, all training at JCI is designed to support the company's strategies and objectives, and processes are in place to make sure everyone understands the connections all along the value chain. Training managers are now proactive; they go out and meet with the heads of each department to find out what their key initiatives and goals are, and their job is to help these managers reach those goals through whatever development means are necessary.

"Members of the account management team are responsible for building the relationship with specific business units and educating themselves about their strategic plans, initiatives, and goals," says Simmons. But it all started with Simmons taking the time and making the effort to educate herself about the company's strategic direction and priorities. Otherwise, none of it would have happened.

The job and duty of every learning professional, especially ones who are relatively new to the role, is to plug themselves into their own organizational conversation as deeply as possible. Doing so is the only way to understand where the organization has been and where it is going. It's also the only way to understand the various dynamics and tensions in play when the CEO makes a decision and others, including you, must get behind it.

The Value of Learning: CEOs vs. CLOs

In 2005, ASTD and IBM conducted a joint study of corporate-level decision makers from 26 companies in 10 different industries to find out about their perspectives on learning's relationship to business strategy. One of the questions asked was, "How does the learning function provide strategic value?" Table 4-2 compares the responses of the CLOs with those of other executives (CEOs, COOs, chief financial officers).

The differences in their responses were striking. Although all the executives agreed on learning's role in strategic enablement, the emphasis on other values is a bit different. Actually, the CLOs are the ones that mention such pragmatic words as "business," "performance," and "efficiency." The other decision makers use such words as "transformation," "innovation," "growth," and "leadership"—precisely the opposite of what one would expect. Aren't the corporate-suite people the ones who are so focused on business issues and numbers that they don't give learning the credit it deserves? Aren't learning professionals the

Table 4-2. Role of the learning function as seen by CLOs and by other executives.

	Strategic Values	Comments
CLOs	• Performance improvement • Strategic enablement • Business unit enablement • Learning operation and efficiency • Talent management	• "Learning will engage early to analyze and improve the design of jobs and processes and technology-based performance support tools." • "Learning can help achieve all the critical success factors for our company, not just the people factors." • "Our workforce management process ensures that we have the best people at the optimal price in place."
Other Executives (CEOs, chief operating officers, chief financial officers)	• Capability building • Transformation • Innovation • Personal growth • Strategic enablement • Leadership development • Globalization	• "Learning helps us develop bench strength and the competencies needed for the future." • "Learning's role is to build the platform to enable us to change the business." • "The learning function's role is to help our company learn, adopt, adapt, and grow."

Source: B. Sugrue, T.O. O'Driscoll, and M.K. Vona, *C-Level Perceptions of the Strategic Value of Learning Research Report* (Alexandria, VA: American Society for Training & Development, 2006).

ones who refuse to face business realities and are preoccupied with learning's impact on the organizational soul? Or, might this be a case of each side telling the other what it wants to hear?

It's hard to tell, but the good news revealed by this study is that business leaders and learning professionals may not be as far apart in their thinking as previously supposed. Both see strategic enablement as a key value driver of learning, and both seem to recognize that learning can play an important role at all levels of the organization. The real "difference" is that the non-CLO executives get to declare what they *want* learning to accomplish, and CLOs and everyone else involved in learning are responsible for delivering it. Results must also be delivered in ways that top-level executives want it.

Whatever else you do, your most important job is understanding the organization's vision, strategy, and objectives as deeply and thoroughly as corporate-level management, so that you can bring value to the organization through learning and development initiatives that help make the CEO's vision a reality.

Better Learning Through Strategic Communication

Focusing on communication issues can open up opportunities for realigning an organization to be more focused, efficient, and effective in executing its strategic objectives. Following are a number of ways learning professionals can help steer their organization in the right direction:

- *Generate support from the top.* Strategically speaking, the most important thing to have in learning is support from the top. Leadership that values learning invests in learning. If not, learning tends to be confined to a tightly sealed box out of which it is almost impossible to escape. However, a high proportion of organizations land somewhere in between; they are not yet aware of learning's full potential but remain open to discussion. Keep the dialog going and specifically target the person or people you need to persuade because they could very well be the keys to your future.

- *Facilitate a more transparent dialog with upper management.* Don't let senior-level managers issue edicts from their office. Get them involved by engaging them as subject matter experts or thought leaders. Ask them to address groups personally about issues they are knowledgeable about. See them as caretakers of the enterprise's core messages, and encourage them to articulate that message as often as possible, to as many people as possible.

Case Study: IBM

Understanding Mission and Values

Taking the time to study and understand an organization's mission and value statements is the first principle of aligned communication because the one person who cares the most about the mission statement is the president or CEO. Whether you are an employee, consultant, or coach, it makes sense to know something about what's important to the person who ultimately signs your paycheck. The CEO has the responsibility of fulfilling an organization's mission, and the standard he or she is judged by is whether or not this fulfillment is happening. Even if you know nothing else about the CEO, you can deduce some of the logic behind his or her decision-making process by knowing what sort of mission and values he or she is supposed to be upholding. And, if you know how a company articulates its core mission and values, you stand a much better chance of understanding its decision chains.

At IBM, for instance, the mission statement is remarkably clear: "At IBM, we strive to lead in the invention, development, and manufacture of the industry's most advanced information technologies, including computer systems, software, storage systems, and microelectronics. We translate these advanced technologies into value for our customers through our professional solutions, services, and consulting businesses worldwide."

The company's statement of values reads as follows: "Our actions will be driven by these values:

- dedication to every client's success
- innovation that matters, for our company and for the world
- trust and personal responsibility in all relationships.

On the surface, this sounds like boilerplate business-speak—the sort of feel-good values for which every company claims to stand. If you were making a presentation in front of IBM CEO Samuel Palmasino, however, it might help to know how these three bullet points were decided upon: In 2005, because of the accelerating nature of change in its markets, as well as the company's increasingly global reach, Palmasino decided it was necessary, for the first time since the company was founded, to examine the fundamental principles that bind IBMers together as a company. Palmasino explains, "Given the realities of a smart, global, independent-minded, 21st-century workforce like ours, I don't believe something as vital and personal as values can be dictated from the top." Consequently, Palmasino invited all 319,000 IBM employees worldwide to engage in a three-day "values jam" on the company's intranet. People were free to say whatever was on their mind, good or bad, and the purpose of the exercise was to determine what values IBM employees really stood for. After sifting through all the responses from tens of thousands of people, the strongest points of consensus were distilled into the three bullet points you read.

Because Palmasino himself didn't invent these values—they were written through a collaborative process involving the entire company—they are extremely important to him. "I feel that I've been handed something every CEO craves: a mandate, for exactly the right kinds of transformation, from an entire workforce," says Palmasino. These values, he believes, are his marching orders. Since these values were posted, Palmasino has in fact made a number of important decisions based entirely on the strength of those three bullet points. IBM's procedures for measuring rewards and performance have changed because of the focus on trust, and the company is making sincere efforts to unburden itself from layers of entrenched bureaucracy. In February of 2006, the board of directors also instituted changes in executive compensation that require the company's stock to rise at least 10 percent per year before executives can realize any profit from their own stock options.

The value in knowing all of this is that it gives you at least a few clues about what makes the president of IBM tick. Whether you work for him or are trying to get some of his business from the outside, this information could serve as a useful foundation for understanding what IBM's current priorities are. If you are a consultant who specializes in integrating and aligning corporate values, you could garner some ideas about how to approach the company with solutions to the problems that arise when one tries to get thousands of people to adhere to the same core values. If you are a learning professional inside the organization, it might shed some light on places in the organization that need realignment with the newly stated values. In any case, this knowledge could help you shape your various communications—phone calls, emails, meetings—in ways that align directly with what the CEO has publicly declared are among his top priorities.

■ *Take responsibility for your own messages.* Make sure the messages you are delivering align with the messages issuing from the top. If you encounter contradictions or confusion, don't hesitate to seek clarification even if you feel as if you are asking a stupid question. In most cases, it's more stupid not to ask. Make sure your goals and objectives complement the organization's, and work toward synergies as often as possible.

■ *Map communication chains to anticipate problem areas.* Use an organizational chart to map how information is flowing through the organization, up and down the chain of command and from side to side. Use the map to identify bottlenecks, points of confusion, counterproductive alliances, redundancies, inefficiencies, and any other type of communication problems. For each type of information (strategic, tactical, informative, personal, or technical), there should be a clear communication path from the CEO all the way down to the customer and all points in between. The message at each stage should be clear and consistent, reflecting the branding and values of the organization.

■ *Identify communications skills gaps that should be filled through training.* Communication failures can often be linked to shortcomings in other areas of an organization. For example, if as part of the meeting and planning process there is no agreed-upon methodology for following up on action items or holding people accountable for what they say they are going to do, things that were supposed to happen will fall through the cracks, important initiatives will get put on the back burners, and momentum in some areas will simply grind to a halt. Training can address such problems by identifying them in the first place and working with the appropriate managers and teams to develop a viable solution. The results of newly established communication threads should be tracked and compared against what would or wouldn't have happened if that communication didn't take place.

- *Emphasize metrics that matter.* Meaningful measurements are different for every organization, but they all have one thing in common: They are defined by the CEO or another executive who's in charge of learning and performance issues. When presenting learning, it makes no sense to offer data that is not directly relevant and meaningful to executives. Use business language and provide the data that answers their specific questions, not yours.

- *Use measurements wisely to benchmark progress.* Measurements don't exist just to prove that progress is being made; they also exist to give team members some basis for comparing their performance against some established norm. Be candid about exactly what is going to be measured and why, and get team members to buy into the idea that measurements are not punitive; they are just one tool among many for tracking progress.

- *Set realistic expectations and then exceed them.* Part of delivering great results is managing expectations beforehand. Do not commit to overly ambitious expectations. Don't promise 100 percent growth if 20 or 30 percent will get the job done. Goals for learning should stretch you and your team's talents but still be within reach.

■ *Become an outsourcing expert.* The reality of business today is that many routine HR and training functions are being outsourced, leaving smaller core groups inside companies to manage learning strategy and balance inside and outside resources. If your goal is to be a strategic asset to your company, it is a wise idea to transform yourself into an out-sourcing expert—the go-to person who knows where to get what from whom in the outside world. Knowing the internal and external worlds is a must.

■ *Pick the right medium for the message.* No one likes to learn via email that they've been laid off or via the morning news that their CEO has been indicted. Effective communication is about delivering the right message through the appropriate medium to the people who need to hear it. Sometimes that means deciding which way will preserve everyone's dignity, even if it's the most direct and uncomfortable way. Choosing the coward's way out for difficult messages sends an even more alarming message to everyone who is "spared." No mat-ter how devastating the message is, if you take care to deliver it in the most respectful, humane way possible, the anguish will pay off in the respect you receive and the sleep you are able to get at night.

■ *Emphasize future value, not past results.* Unless you have a stellar record to draw upon or credible and impressive meas-urements to document learning's past contributions, focus discussions on the value you can bring in the future. A busi-ness's challenges are in front of it, not behind it, and the past should be learned from but not necessarily repeated. Part of the reason for understanding a business's dynamics so thor-oughly and for developing the ability to talk about learning's impact in the language of business is being able to help lead-ers imagine how an investment in learning will help the organization grapple with the unknowns ahead.

■ *Focus on needs and results, not activity.* Too many learning professionals focus on activity data such as how many courses have been taken or how many hours of training per employee they are delivering. Business managers want to see the impact of learning in terms of addressing the needs of the organization, and they want evidence of results.

■ *Build credibility slowly.* A sense of reliability and credibility are qualities that are built over time, for they are essentially elements of trust. Throwing out huge ROI figures for learning initiatives is more likely to engender skepticism than enthusiasm. Far more convincing is a record of consistent success, coupled with a reputation for honesty and an ability to talk about the value of learning in real-world business language. Deliver early and small wins and build upon the momentum generated.

■ *Learn best practices from others.* One sure way to light a competitive fire or two is to keep abreast of best practices at other organizations. When the time is right, you can say, "Look, they're doing it this way, and getting these results, which are better than ours." This works especially well when the "they" you are referring to happens to be your closest competition.

■ *Have faith in training, but don't be afraid to admit the truth.* Everyone has a surface faith in the importance of training, but the sad truth is that despite everyone's best intentions, some learning efforts are ill-advised, ineffective, boring, counterproductive, and sometimes downright silly—in general, a waste of time, money, and resources. When a program fails, don't be afraid to admit it. Learn from those mistakes and move on with a greater commitment to providing content the organization really needs.

One common thread in all the pointers offered above is the critical importance of using communication to engage decision makers in organizational learning to ensure alignment of your learning initiatives with your organization's goals and the strategies to achieve those goals. So important is this concept that ASTD has developed several criteria related to executive engagement and strategic alignment for selecting organizations to receive its annual prestigious BEST awards. The ASTD BEST Awards recognize organizations that demonstrate enterprisewide success as a result of employee learning and development. Award winners show that they are BEST at **B**uilding talent, **E**nterprisewide, **S**upported by the organization's leaders, fostering a **T**horough learning culture. The BEST organizations are ones that can provide metrics and evidence of strong links between learning activities and business results that are strategically important to the company and are able to show learning's relevance to organizational goals.

Very Important Points

- Ultimately, communication is what demonstrates the link between an organization's business objectives and its learning programs and initiatives. Therefore, it's important to make accurate, effective communication a top strategic priority.

- Presentations are the primary form of professional communication, but learning professionals need to broaden their thinking about what constitutes a presentation.

- Almost every interaction you have with others during the business day, whether formal or informal, is a presentation of sorts.

- Aligning communications in an organization will almost automatically align learning, especially if everyone understands that effective presentations of all kinds can be a vital strategic asset.

- Analyzing how communication affects or detracts from organizational strategy can open up all kinds of opportunities for learning to assert itself.

- Building a strong alliance with HR can be an important strategic move, because the field shares many of the same challenges, and has many of the same goals.

This chapter presented some striking findings from the ASTD/IBM study of how top-level executives on both sides of the organizational learning fence view the role of workplace learning. Everyone seems to understand that workplace learning professionals must ensure that their goals dovetail with the organization's business strategy as envisioned by the CEO. You also read a couple of case studies showing how this unified focus can bring real bottom-line results measured in business terms. One tangible way to help bring this about is for the workplace learning professional to forge an alliance with the HR function.

The next chapter delves more deeply into the SPEAK model, showing how to use the personalization component to communicate to corporate executives about the value of workplace learning, using measures that they embrace.

Creating and Presenting Value

To the Point

t's great to have data and measurements to support the claim that learning adds value to the enterprise, but value can be communicated in a number of different ways. One of the most effective ways to persuade top-level executives that training has value on the balance sheet and beyond is to get them involved in it as either participants or subject matter experts through the power of persuasion. Indeed, an important part of Presentation Mastery is knowing how to cultivate and leverage personal relationships to get the outcomes you want. This is part of the power of personalization, one of three *P*s of the SPEAK model introduced in chapter 3.

The process of presenting a persuasive case for learning is often thought of as one or more people trying to convince their superiors to accept the wisdom of a given initiative and give it their blessing. Often, however, the most persuasive way to communicate the value of learning to upper executives is to get them involved in it as either participants or instructors. Once upper executives see and, more important, feel the value of workplace learning in action, they often become evangelists who have the power to transform entire organizations.

One of the Wal-Mart Ways

In the 1990s, Cole Peterson was the executive vice president for HR, one of the top five positions at Wal-Mart. During his time with the corporation, Wal-Mart became the world's largest company, growing from 300,000 to 1.5 million employees. Early in his tenure, the company's CEO, Lee Scott, worried that communication was breaking down somewhere along the chain of command and suspected that the company's managers were at fault. Peterson says his marching orders were, "We've got to improve the skills of management around here."

Rather than assess the problem, develop a solution, and deploy it, however, Peterson told the executive committee that he could do what they asked, but that he couldn't do it unless they all agreed to participate and lead the way. "I told them that I'd like to develop a high-level development process, but that all of us had to go through our own two-day assessment first," recalls Peterson. There was some initial resistance, but Peterson wore them down. "I told them that we could develop the best training and development process in the world, but if we had poor strategy, lousy execution, and indifferent leadership, it wasn't going to work."

"It all comes down to leadership," says Peterson. "What's happening in a lot of organizations today is that the people running them think leadership's role is to delegate training. But that sends the wrong message. If you want training to work, leaders have to participate in it and demonstrate to everyone else that they believe in it. If they don't commit to it, leaders below them will feel no obligation to commit or invest in it, either."

Peterson ended up getting his way, and the entire executive leadership of Wal-Mart went through a rigorous two-day assessment of their leadership, management, and communication skills. The results, says Peterson, were dramatic: "After we all got assessed, we talked about our feedback and shared it with others. We made it into a fun thing by playing off of each other in meetings. Our CEO's development task was sarcasm so we had a lot of fun with that, and the managers who worked for us saw us having fun. They also saw us seriously trying to implement some of the communication strategies that we had learned. It was very powerful. How could my direct reports not take training seriously when they see all of us, at the top, talking about our own experience? The answer is, they can't, and they didn't, and the program was a huge success."

What Is Your Value?

Communicating value in their everyday presentations is not always so easy for learning professionals. Many do not comprehend fully how valuable they are to their organizations. They have difficulty putting a dollar value on their contribution. They struggle gauging the effect of their efforts on the bottom line or any other line, for that matter. They search for a holistic, systemic view of how knowledge flows and multiplies in an organization. They feel and know in their hearts that they are contributing *something* (because how can learning be bad, right?), and their primary evidence for this is that people seem to like the training.

Unfortunately, because so few learning professionals know how to define their value, they have not set a high priority on communicating it to their colleagues, superiors, clients, or anyone else. As a Presentation Master, this is not for you. For you, communicating your value isn't just a priority, it's a strategic imperative. It's the flipside of creating value, and these two essential practices—creating value and effectively presenting it—are what distinguish high-performing Masters from the also-rans.

Business Simulation Communicates the Value of Intangibles

To communicate the value of intangibles, Computer Sciences Corporation has a course entitled, "The Business Leader Workshop." It's a business simulation course in which managers run a knowledge-based company at an enterprise level and in a competitive market. By exercising executive-level decisions in response to various business pressures and market conditions over the course of six years of operations management, they began to see their decisions pay off, ultimately, in the business value of intangibles such as training. They might not be able to quantify what they've learned, but by participating in the exercise and receiving feed-back from their coach and peers, they know intuitively that the training is valuable because they can see its affect on themselves. To capitalize on those realizations, the company's learning department developed a campaign with the slogan, "Leaders never stop learning," to reinforce the idea that as people move through their careers, they should continually fine-tune their leadership skills and keep building on them.

Creating Value

Unlike those who don't know their own value or how to articulate it, great communicators are keenly aware of the value they bring to the table. Not only do they know how to create the value that confers a seat at the table, they know how to communicate that value in all their presentations. One of the biggest side benefits of knowing what your value is, however, is that it frees your mind to look for opportunities to *create even more value,* and that, too, is something at which Presentation Masters excel.

In previous chapters, we have emphasized the idea that presentations are not just stand-and-deliver events that happen every now and then; presentation situations—the occasions when you communicate your ideas, values, beliefs, and wishes to other human beings—occur all the time, every day, in the form of meetings, phone calls, emails, casual

Changing With the Times at Wal-Mart

The obvious place to start when trying to determine the value of learning is with the question of what to measure and how. But, according to Cole Peterson, who spent 10 years of his career as executive vice president of HR for Wal-Mart, many learning organizations and practitioners get it wrong right out of the chute by failing to follow their own advice.

"In training and HR, unfortunately, we often fall victim to the very things we want to teach," says Peterson. "For example, we're always talking about setting goals and measuring outcomes, but when you sit down and talk about the goals of trainers, or the training department in general, their goals are obtuse and unclear."

Peterson was ahead of his time at Wal-Mart, where he long ago implemented a proactive, needs-based approach to learning. His advice to those who really want to make a difference in their organizations is to focus on developing solid working relationships with line managers—the people for whom effective training of personnel is most essential—and don't impose your beliefs about what's "needed" onto anyone; let them tell you.

"The people who are winning the battle are those who can get the line manager involved in the development of training, and who have ability to get metrics agreed upon beforehand," says Peterson. "It's not enough to be smart, to know a lot, or to be certified. If you can't motivate a line manager to be your partner, you're not going to get anywhere."

According to Peterson, the other major factor limiting the effectiveness of many learning professionals is a stubborn refusal to change with the times. "We as training pros, even when we change companies, have the same fix-it tools, the same bag of tricks. They're things we're comfortable with and know how to implement. Consequently, lots of people don't want to go to a line manager and say, 'Let's do a diagnosis of your needs,' because it might mean that they have to do something different. They might have to learn another method or hire someone from the outside to do it."

conversations, and so on. We've also been reinforcing the theme that preparing for presentations is not something Presentation Masters just do every now and then either; they are constantly collecting magazine and journal articles, book references, anecdotes, stories, facts, data, charts, testimonials, and other information they can use to support their cause, whatever that may be. They keep this information organized by subject matter or other content category, in both paper and electronic form, so that it is available to them whenever they need it. Furthermore, they don't just file it and forget it. If they want to use an anecdote that illustrates the importance of time management, say, they will practice it on several different types of people, noting the responses of each, before they ever use it in front of a group. In presentation situations, this combination of foresight, organization, practice, and discipline gives them a distinct advantage over their peers.

Communicating value is something else that Masters do not dabble in occasionally; they do it frequently, in several different ways, few of which involve trotting out ROI calculations or pulling up a spreadsheet.

One of the most powerful ways in which Presentation Masters convey their value to the people they are working with or for is *by actually being valuable!* They don't just do their jobs well and achieve their goals; they do everything in their power to help other people reach their goals. Like everything else Presentation Masters do, however, they do it with both a plan and purpose in mind.

SPEAK to Win

When thinking about the communication of value in an enterprise, it's helpful to go back to the SPEAK model introduced in chapter 3. As the circular design of the model suggests (figure 5-1), Presentation Masters engage in continual, self-reinforcing cycles of communication that revolve around a win-win mindset. By looking for and finding solutions that are beneficial to all parties involved, people who operate at level 3 of the presentation impact curve—the Presentation

Figure 5-1. The SPEAK model.

Masters who make the most of their mind, personal network, influence, abilities, and resources—are able to generate a great deal of positive momentum. As this momentum picks up speed, it naturally attracts the energy of people who want to go in a similar direction, which is one of the reasons that Presentation Master so often end up in leadership positions.

In terms of their ability to create value or the perception of value, the most underestimated (and overlooked) piece of the puzzle has to do with personal relationships. People often say it's "who you know" that is important, and executives sometimes joke that they're only as valuable as their Rolodex organizer, and there is some truth in both of these observations. In the world of Presentation Mastery, however, it's not only whom you know that counts, it's how you cultivate, nurture, and maintain relationships that matters.

It's difficult to overstate how important the quality of one's personal relationships is to his or her overall effectiveness and success in the field of workplace learning and performance. You can have a desk full of assessments and ROI figures testifying to the value of a program, but if you don't have constructive relationships with key decision makers, your ideas, no matter how good they are, may go nowhere. Likewise, if you have a friendly personal relationship with the chief operating officer who has confidence in your judgment and generally supports what you do, piles of self-justifying paperwork may be unnecessary.

We're not saying that you should abandon your value-measurement efforts to go work on your golf swing. What we are saying is that in the real world, where a premium is put on being able to get things done and make things happen, learning how to work with and through other people is an essential and often underappreciated skill. To an enormous degree, how you manage your everyday relationships and interactions with people determines what you are able to accomplish. Presentation Masters know this, which is why they treat their Rolodex—their network of friends, associates, and acquaintances—not just as a bunch of people they happen to know but as a vital strategic asset.

By strategic, we simply mean that Presentation Masters are consciously aware of the inherent value of their personnel network, so they do not waste or squander it; they use it to their fullest advantage. What does this mean? And, how do you take advantage of people without actually *taking advantage* of them? Those are the Presentation Mastery secrets we'd like to share with you now.

Win With Win-Win

At the center of the SPEAK model are the words "win win," with revolving arrows indicating that the process is ongoing and continuous. These words are in the middle of the circle because the win-win mindset is at the center of much of what Presentation Masters do.

Presentation Masters are constantly looking for ways to negotiate win-win situations in which both parties feel as if they got something valuable. This feeling is important because people hate being taken advantage of. Conversely, they love feeling that they got a good deal. The trouble with solutions that don't have a win-win framework is that someone ends up feeling like a loser. When people lose, especially competitive people, they get angry, and angry people can do a great deal of damage in an organization. If you win a negotiation but the other party feels manipulated or outmaneuvered, you end up sending a ball of negative energy hurtling throughout the organization, one that can gather force and come back to haunt you. It's ultimately self-defeating. That's why Presentation Masters, even if they can see a way to get what they want without giving anything up, will continue to search for a way to make the other party feel as if they have received something valuable out of the deal. Why? Because in the long term, it is much more advantageous to have allies than enemies, and negotiations of all types are opportunities to solidify personal relationships that might pay off in the future.

This is what's strategic about the way Presentation Masters work. They do not see interactions (presentations) with other people as isolated, separate events; they see them as touch-points in a continuous, self-reinforcing cycle of communication. Ask most CLOs in large companies what they actually do all day, and it will have little to do with learning per se. It will have everything to do with "relationship-building," "sales," "marketing," and "bridge-building," which are the most common organizational terms for *presenting to and influencing other people.*

Now, most people prefer win-win solutions when they can find them. Where Presentation Masters differ from other people is that they make a personal mission out of finding them. When Presentation Masters listen, one of the main things they listen for is opportunities to help the person they are talking to achieve an objective or goal. Helping people help each other through the workplace learning function makes good business sense. The reason it makes good business sense is a concept that social scientists call the reciprocity rule.

The Rule of Reciprocity

With its basis in the Platinum Rule ("Do unto others as they would like have done unto them"), the rule of reciprocity has been extrapolated by psychologist Robert Cialdini (2006) to serve as a foundation for effective persuasion in any number of contexts. The reciprocity rule is an involuntary psychological response that kicks in when people receive a gift or when someone does a favor for them. When people receive such a gift or favor, people feel compelled to do something of equal value in return for the gift or favor they have received.

In one famous experiment, diners at a restaurant were monitored for how much they tipped the waiter. Some diners simply got their check, while others got their check *plus* a couple of chocolate pieces. Even though they had received the same service and food, diners who received the chocolates tipped consistently more than those who did not receive the chocolates. The reason: They had received something unexpected free (the chocolates), and they compensated by tipping one or two percent more than they would have normally. This is why most restaurants now bring a candy, dinner mint, or some other treat along with the check. It is also why maids leave chocolates on the pillows of hotel guests; the reciprocity principle compels guests to leave larger tips.

Although people may feel an impulse to reciprocate when they receive something from someone, the reciprocity rule doesn't mean that people will actually *do* something in return, but it does mean that given the opportunity to reciprocate, they will probably try to do so. Presentation Masters use this principle to their advantage by seeding goodwill wherever they can. The payoff may not happen this week or this month, but Masters know that dividends will come to them in both expected and unexpected forms, and they have faith in the principle that "what goes around comes around." It doesn't have to take a great deal of time, either. For example, if you know two people who are working on similar or complementary projects but don't know each other, it only takes about 10 seconds to send an email to each person to introduce them electronically. Nothing may come of it, but if the two people involved do contact each other and they are able to work together somehow, they both will feel a sense of gratitude to you for introducing them. Down the road, these people may repay that gratitude in a hundred different ways, none of which you can predict or count on, but seeding or "banking" all of that positive energy often pays off big time.

Evidence for this connectedness can be found in many places. Malcolm Gladwell (2005) points out that people who habitually connect people they know with each other or who are good at fitting people they just met into the context of their own network, are known as "connectors." In knowledge networks, connectors are the ones who accelerate and multiply the breadth and value of knowledge, so being a connector in a learning enterprise is paramount. Connectors are also extremely good at building alliances between themselves and others, alliances that are essential for operating effectively in any organization, particularly large ones in which the power is distributed in several different directions and competing for influence goes with the territory. The more alliances you build—that is, the more people who support you, especially at the higher levels of the organization—the more power you will have to influence outcomes.

Crack the Toughest Nuts

Another alliance-building strategy that Presentation Masters use to create win-win scenarios is called "cracking the toughest nut." The 80-20 rule comes into play here. The idea is that if 80 percent of your problems are caused by 20 percent of the people, the strategic thing to do is target the 20 percent who are giving you problems, win them over, and, in turn, 80 percent of your problems will disappear. Another axiom that applies is: "Hold your friends close and your enemies closer."

Often, only one or two people stand in the way of a proposal. The "crack the toughest nut" theory means that if you can win over the person most likely to stand in your way, your job is going to be much easier. Targeting them, finding out what their points of resistance are, and then working to resolve them amicably will yield larger dividends per unit of your time than working on other people. Besides, winning over an adversary can be one of the most rewarding experiences in professional life.

One paradox of the toughest nut is that once cracked, the tough nuts can become your staunchest allies. When that happens, you not only neutralize the problem once posed by this person, you multiply the gain by converting them into a champion. CLO David Vance at Caterpillar had just such an experience with one of his colleagues, a man who for a long time seemed to dislike him. "We disagreed on everything," recalls Vance. "For a long time, it was almost painful to talk to him, but then something strange happened. At some point, because we disagreed so often, we started to respect each other more. Then we started to get to know each other, and things suddenly became much easier."

Paying close attention to your strongest critics can also yield valuable information that you can use to pull fence-sitters your way. What's valuable about strong critics is that they are not afraid to tell you the truth as they see it, and this insight can help you understand why others in the organization might be resisting albeit less vehemently. If your detractor is someone who is relatively high up in the organization, for instance, he or she likely has a network of allies who think along the same lines. In such cases, insight into one person's thinking can give you clues about the thinking of dozens of other people as well.

Let Programs Sell Themselves

An excellent way to achieve win-wins and communicate value, particularly intangible value that is difficult to quantify, is to mobilize organizational leaders to participate in the training process; to involve them as conduits for the knowledge they want to deliver, and harness them as witnesses, converts, and champions. It's the difference between telling customers about a new product and letting them try it for themselves. In the end, *you* don't end up selling the program; *they* wind up selling the program to *themselves.*

Getting busy executives to participate in learning isn't always easy, especially if those at the top are skeptical or unaware of training's value to begin with. But, that's also why it's so important to get them involved because the ultimate effectiveness of all learning in an enterprise is often determined by attitudes and behaviors at the top. If your CEO is the toughest nut you have to crack, you have your work cut out for you. But, if you do succeed, it can transform an indifferent culture into a culture where learning is valued and where the value of learning can spread.

Very Important Points

- One of the most persuasive ways to communicate the value of learning is to involve people, especially executives, in the learning and development process either through direct participation or teaching as a subject matter expert.

- Make a priority out of knowing what your value to an organization is and how to communicate what you're worth.

- Creating and communicating value should be strategic imperatives.

- Build your presentation arsenal with stories, anecdotes, magazine articles, book references, data, and charts. But don't file them and forget them; practice using this material, especially stories and anecdotes, in front of different audiences to see how they react.

- Strong personal relationships are paramount, but it's not just whom you know that counts—it's how you cultivate, nurture, and maintain relationships that matters.

- Always strive for win-win solutions, even if it takes more work. The payoff is in seeding goodwill and positive energy rather than making people angry and potentially turning them into enemies.

- Always listen for opportunities to help someone else achieve their goals. Help them if you can, even if you aren't getting anything directly out of it.

- The reciprocity rule is a psychological impulse that kicks in when people receive a gift or favor; it makes them want to do favors in return. Use this principle to seed goodwill and positive momentum throughout your organization.

- Targeting and cracking "the toughest nuts" are effective ways to clear obstacles that may stand in the way of you and your goals.

- Listen to your toughest critics; they can usually teach you something.

This chapter offered some practical advice about the how Presentation Masters can capitalize on the personalization component of the SPEAK model. The next chapter offers more specifics about communicating with a very important audience—the CEO.

Understanding Your Friendly Neighborhood CEO

To the Point

The most important factor in learning's impact on any organization is consistent support from the top. Without that support, the job of learning professionals becomes much more difficult and much less rewarding. One of the important skills that 21st-century learning professionals need to develop is the ability to articulate learning's impact on the organization in terms top executives understand and appreciate. Understanding how CEOs think about business challenges, management issues, and training's role in the organization is the first step toward being able to win their confidence and support.

Many learning professionals, including outside consultants, aspire to be strategic business partners who sit at the table of leadership, where all the important decisions about the direction and management of the business are made, and where it is decided how resources are going to be allocated. For learning professionals to assert themselves and their discipline as a valuable strategic asset, they must find ways to contribute more creatively and effectively to the execution of the organization's mission, and they must become more adept at communicating their influence up and down the organization.

The chief frustration of many learning professionals is the constant demand for proof that learning is making a difference, that it is somehow *adding value* to the organization. CEOs want to see concrete evidence that something happened in that classroom or on that computer that moved the organization forward in some way. They also want to know whether training encouraged some sort of behavioral change in people. Are they doing their jobs better? Are they using their time efficiently? Are they selling more? Has a process been streamlined? Do the people who took the training think they got anything out of it? Have the customers noticed any improvement? Has the number of service complaints gone down?

"I don't think the role of teacher is optional in today's complex, multifunctional, multinational, technology organization. It's part of the job. And it's a fun part."

—Ed Ludwig, president and CEO,
Becton, Dickinson & Co.

Senior executives want this evidence because these factors correlate with the standards by which *they* are judged. CEOs don't have to justify the existence of the training department to anyone; they just want assurance that the training function is working as effectively and efficiently as it can, and that it's doing what it's supposed to do. If it isn't, it's their job to mess with it until it does. If you can't show them what changes have taken place because of the training, then you are not representing them well. If you don't have the evidence to present to them, they can't turn around and show it to the people who are looking over *their* shoulder, the board of directors and the shareholders.

In general, organizational leaders must satisfy these four basic constituencies:

1. *Shareholders and investors:* In publicly held companies especially, providing a consistent rate of economic return for shareholders is job number one. Giving Wall Street analysts something positive to talk about is closely related. Sometimes, short-term fixes (such as sudden cuts to the training budget) that don't make long-term sense happen because a number at the top needs to be hit. Also, a CEO's compensation is usually tied in some significant way to the value delivered to the shareholders or investors, so—though it may sound cynical—following the money trail can give you some insight about the outside factors influencing decisions at the top.

2. *Customers:* For an organization to thrive, its customers must be satisfied with what they are getting. Happy customers generally mean that an organization is doing things right, so leaders tend to pay close attention to what customers are saying. Positive customer response also gives leaders a mandate to do what they want and confidence that their leadership is on the right track. If you can find ways to make customers happier, not just employees, someone upstairs is going to take notice. Customer satisfaction often is treated as a leading indicator—happy customers buy more and more often.

3. *The organization:* Organizational health is one of a CEO's primary concerns because without it, organizations slowly succumb to the business equivalents of cancer: declining productivity, dysfunctional leadership, and disengaged employees. Healthy organizations are ones in which employee engagement is high because everyone is committed to the same

goals, where organizational knowledge translates into the right kind of innovation to meet changing market demands, and where the leadership is trusted to make the right decisions for the future. Organizational culture is difficult to manage, however, especially if it isn't working very well. Progressive leaders know that if they get the culture right, the business is likely to fall in place as well. That's why learning professionals who want to make a difference can often do so effectively by providing ways to create and enrich the desired culture, and to ensure that when positions need to be filled, they are done so in positive ways that enhance institutional knowledge.

4. *Employees:* Raising awareness at the top about the importance of investing in individual skills to improve the overall capability of the workforce is a goal every learning professional should embrace. Ultimately, the performance of any organization, including its value to customers and shareholders, is a function of the collective effort of its skilled, agile, and engaged employees. The goal of workplace learning is to ensure that staff has the right skills at the right time for the right job.

The Reality

From where the CEO sits, all four constituencies are top priorities. Depending on the circumstances, however, the order of those priorities may shift, and learning has a way of getting lost in the shuffle.

"From the CEO's perspective, training is just one tool for getting the performance and results they want," says Bob Prosen, president of the Prosen Center for Business Advancement. Prosen and his research team have surveyed hundreds of CEOs across the country, in dozens of different industries, about their views on leadership and learning. Although shades of opinion vary, says Prosen, some common threads run through the views of those in the top office.

"The fact is that businesses—particularly public companies—are primarily interested in performance and profit," explains Prosen. "It

"I think the CEO has to be personally involved and personally committed to leadership development. One of the things we're working on is establishing a desired culture. We want to create an expectation around behavior, and that behavior had better start here with me."

—Mark J. Schwab, CEO and president,
Binney & Smith

sounds cold, but that's the reality. So, it stands to reason that anything that supports performance and profit is going to be looked upon more favorably. People are an important part of that equation, so you have to treat them right, develop and challenge them, and make sure they're in positions they love. But it's up to the people in those jobs to make sure the training they receive gets used and is reflected in their job performance."

CEOs also tend to see training as serving two basic functions for an enterprise, says Prosen: "First, they want training to help employees develop and get more engaged and proficient at what they do. That's the broad benefit. Then there's focused training on specific job functions and processes. . . where they expect to see a measurable increase in performance and profit."

The case for a basic level of training is not difficult to make, says Prosen, because most leaders recognize that some level of training is necessary to keep an organization going. Precisely what that level is can vary, says Prosen, because the line between nice-to-haves and need-to-haves moves in relation to the health of the economy and how well the organization is faring against its competitors.

"Unfortunately, when budgets get tight, what are the first things to get cut? Marketing and training. Why? Because decision makers don't see them as being connected directly to the bottom line. People who are in danger of being caught in that position should rethink their role in the organization," says Prosen. "Because I guarantee that if you can communicate the results piece—if you can show a CEO [or other executives] how training improved a product development cycle, increased productivity, saved money, or otherwise contributed to the financial success of the organization—they'll listen. If budgets are tight and you start talking to them about feel-good things such as improved morale and teamwork, they won't listen."

Talk Business to Me

Learning professionals often see a single-minded business focus as a kind of management myopia that doesn't allow anyone over the level of a vice president to see the larger picture. CEOs tend to be busy, time-crunched types who want people to get to the point fast. They don't want to hear all the gory details about how you arrived at such-and-such a number or what your whole thought process was going into a project. They just want to know what's important and what isn't, which, when presenting information to them, means you have to cut about 99 percent of what you want to say and get right to the 1 percent that matters. It also means you have to shelve the trainer-speak for the time being and speak to them in plain English or at least business English. CEOs may not know or care about Kirkpatrick's level 1 (learner satisfaction) or level 2 (assessment of learning through testing) evaluation of training, but they know what results look like and they do care about those. Therefore, articulating workplace learning results in conventional business terms is the logical, if not always the easiest, thing to do.

The common wisdom that learning professionals should learn the language of business is a response to the even more common wisdom that learning professionals don't know enough about business. To senior executives, those in the learning trenches sometimes are thought of as soft because they appear to care more about the people they are training than the business they are training them for. This isn't necessarily true, but this perception sometimes hobbles the efforts of those who have not adequately demonstrated their commitment to the business itself before plunging ahead with ambitious but unproven programs for organizational enlightenment.

CEO Support at J.B. Hunt

Trucking giant J.B. Hunt is one of many large companies that has invested a tremendous amount of money in vast catalogs of course content covering every conceivable training and development topic. Such catalogs were quite popular in the late 1990s, when a maturing Internet made it possible to archive astonishing amounts of content online and the prospect of giving employees access to a database to do much of their training "when they want to, at their own pace, on their own" seemed like a great idea. To companies like J.B. Hunt, however, such catalogs started to look like a shot-gun approach to training that wastes money by trying to provide some-thing for everybody. Monty Morton, J.B. Hunt's Director of Training and Development, says the company is now taking a more "strategic, focused" approach to training, one that directs learning resources "where they will do the most good" rather than spreading them out all over the place.

"We were doing e-learning, sure, but we were just buying giant libraries and telling people to go learn," says Morton. The sheer volume of content also became a drawback. "There was so much available that it was over-whelming people," says Morton. "They ended up just putting it off."

Morton's budget for e-learning in 2006 was about the same as it was for 2005; the difference is in how J.B. Hunt is spending the money. "We are a company with homegrown roots and values that is growing relatively fast, so fast that we realized we could no longer count on ensur-ing our leadership succession internally. We need to be able to hire peo-ple out of college and have them managing within a year, so we spent last year defining a 23-point leadership competency model, and now we're creating content around those competencies."

This newly targeted content follows a blended learning model, with customized e-content providing the knowledge foundation and dedicated classroom work putting the online content into action. "In the past, we would have just had them take the course and get the hours," says Morton. "Now we're getting much more out of our e-content by supple-menting it with a classroom environment in which they can try out what they've learned online in a safe environment. The classroom follow-up also introduces accountability because they have to take the online portion before they can do the classroom work. We still have an online catalog, but where we might have had 20 courses for a particular topic before, we might have five now."

J.B. Hunt's top leaders are much happier with the program as well, even though Morton says they are inherently skeptical of any claims of direct ROI. "They're smart enough to know that cause and effect in training may not be what you say or think it is. But, they're generally supportive of training, and the way we're doing it now they can see that it's more targeted and efficient, and they can see a direct connection between the training, how the training translates into practice in the field, and how all of these individual objectives link up with the business's overall strategies."

Don't Talk Like a Trainer

The other big obstacle to communication between top-level executives and learning professionals is a linguistic one. Professional training jargon doesn't travel very well. To anyone unfamiliar with such terms of training art as competency mapping, asynchronous learning, learning initiatives, or blended solutions, it can all be rather daunting. And, if you want to communicate with someone, mystifying them is not the way to go about it. Besides, people tend to fear things they don't understand, which is why the more complicated and detailed a learning evaluation system is, the more likely it is that executives will distrust it. They want the bottom line, and they want it now.

To a highly trained and certified learning professional, however, calculating bottom-line business results entails a standard business investment analysis, which learning professionals, if they are not already doing, need to become very comfortable with.

Ignore the impulse to say, "It's not that simple" and then expound on all the different levels and evaluations and assessments needed to come up with an accurate calculation, and why even those results must be somewhat qualified. What the CEO hears is, "I don't know." CEOs don't understand why it's so difficult to figure out if a learning program

"When our sales are growing, I know we are doing a good job of training. That's exactly how we look at it. We feel that with their knowledge, our people are able to serve our customers in a way they won't be served anywhere else, and that grows our business."

—Dan Wegman, CEO,
Wegman Foods

is working. Did sales go up, yes or no? Is the cycle time shorter, yes or no? Do people know more than they did before, yes or no? Such situations can be very challenging. To communicate effectively with CEOs, then, you will need to learn how to talk to them in their language. The language of business is largely the language of money, results, and other key organizational measures.

Money Talk

Understanding the basics of financial management is a prerequisite for anyone who wants to sit at the table and, once seated, have something useful to contribute. For better or worse, money metrics are the basic language of business, and learning the vocabulary of money is as fundamental to this skill as learning scales, modes, and notation are to a musician.

"In the current business zeitgeist, for learning to have a strategic seat at the table, you have to have a global business understanding and be engaged with the challenges of the business. For example, every [corporate] person's nightmare is the huge demographic shift that's beginning to happen now, with senior management leaving in droves, taking their institutional knowledge with them. Learning has to be involved in meeting those challenges, and helping to solve the profitability puzzle."

—Laura Bernstein, president,
VisionPoint

You need to know how to read a balance sheet; the difference between profit, position, and cash; how revenue, earnings, and profit are calculated; what liquidity and debt-to-equity ratios are; the difference between assets and liabilities; what the acronym EBITDA means (an accountant's term that means earnings before income, taxes, depreciation, and amortization); and, of course, how such measures as ROIC (return-on-invested-capital) and return-on-assets (ROA) are calculated. Ultimately, you also need to know how all of these financial metrics apply to the organization you are working with or for, and their degree of importance at that time for the organization. Specifically, you need to know how they feed into the organization's various value chains and what they mean as far as the organization's overall performance is concerned.

Theresa Seagraves's book, *Quick! Show Me Your Value,* is a great primer on business basics for learning professionals, and it includes several worksheets and templates, including a financial imperatives scorecard for breaking down value propositions into manageable, communicable pieces. In addition, a glossary of terms offers brief definitions of some of the basic business terms learning professionals should know.

Show Me the Results

It's simple, really: CEOs want to know how much things cost, what the money is buying, and what they're getting in return. Results are what executives want to see, and if showing them were easy, everyone's job would be simple. Try to look at it from the CEO's perspective, though. Training is expensive. Plenty of money goes down that tube, and if that money doesn't appear to be buying anything, the logical question is: Do we need to spend it? Table 6-1 presents some of the tough questions that CEOs ask workplace learning professionals.

All CEOs recognize that a certain amount of money must go to training, or the organization will fail to keep up with the marketplace. Where they differ is in how much capital they believe should go into

Table 6-1. Twenty of the toughest questions a CEO can ask a learning professional.

1. Does training deliver any real bottom-line value to the organization?

2. Can you show me, in numbers, what return we're getting for our learning investment?

3. Beyond basic job training, does any extra investment in learning pay off? If so, how?

4. Do our competitors invest more or less than we do in learning?

5. If we do invest more in learning, precisely where will we see the results? How long will it take for results to be visible?

6. Do you have any evidence that further training makes people more productive or that it makes them perform better?

7. Can training make fair employees good or good employees great?

8. Do certain jobs need more training than others? If so, how do you decide which jobs those are and what metrics do you use to track the results?

9. Are we doing the right kind of training? How do you know?

10. What would happen if we just outsourced all of our learning/training?

11. Are we getting the best learning possible for our organization for the money we spend? How do you determine the quality of the training you provide?

12. If we spent our money smarter, could we spend less and get the same results?

13. Is training critical to our organization's success? How so?

14. What do our line managers and employees have to say about the effectiveness of our training efforts? Have we surveyed them?

15. In what ways are we striving to improve our learning efforts?

16. Do we have the best/right people managing and conducting our training?

17. Do you have any evidence that investing in leadership and management training creates better, more loyal managers? Or, are we just training people and handing them over to the competition?

18. Do our learning efforts respond adequately to changing market conditions and competitive pressures? Can you give me an example? Do you have a process for deciding when and what to change?

19. Do we have the right people in the right places with the right skills? If so, how do you know? If not, what are we doing to address the situation?

20. Why do most people hate training but complain that they don't get enough of it?

"We used to apply a 'push' approach to training. Now there's much more of a 'pull' effect. People are saying, 'I have to deliver sustainable business. What do I have to do to get this done?' We've seen a big increase in requests for leadership development and succession planning tools, for example."

—Robert W. Lane, president and CEO,
John Deere & Company

training and in how much faith they have that training is a good investment. Building a strong believer in learning at the top is critical for your success.

In many ways, however, the learning professional's job is showing CEOs certain benefits they cannot immediately see. Learning is like gravity: You can't see it, but you can see its effects, many of which we take for granted. Your job is to get senior executives thinking about the impact of learning on organizational success in new and more appreciative ways.

Who's Accountable?

Accountability is another characteristic that CEOs value very highly. Accountability means taking responsibility for one's own work, making decisions based on a solid business rationale, owning up to mistakes and miscalculations, and not being afraid to have one's effectiveness tracked or measured. If business were baseball, advocates of accountability would want everyone to have the equivalent of a batting average, an ongoing, day-to-day statistical measurement of how everyone is doing compared to his or her own past performance and compared to the competition. Unproductive players cannot hide from a lousy batting average, but unproductive workers can often hide behind all sorts of smokescreens.

Top executives respect anyone who goes to the trouble to make themselves and their departments more accountable. The root word of accountability is "account," after all, so financial measures are at the top

Opportunity May Await You in a Spreadsheet

There are several strategic reasons why being able to converse intelligently about the data in spreadsheets might come in handy for learning professionals. Not only does it give you something to say while you're sitting at the boardroom table and demonstrate your commitment to understanding the business side of things, understanding financial parameters can also help you see new opportunities.

For example, one concern of upper management is making sure that certain ratios—liquidity ratio, debt-to-equity ratio, profit ratio—are where they ought to be. Targets are typically set for each, so if you know what the target is and can recognize if the ratio is out of line with the target, there might be an opportunity hidden in the discrepancy. If you can envision a way for learning to influence the number—by knowing what that number says about the performance of the organization leading up to it—and can convince those around the table that a learning initiative will help, you will have accomplished four objectives at once:

- You will have gained the respect of management for even recognizing the problem in the first place.
- You will have demonstrated how learning can affect the business in a positive, tangible way.
- You will have connected the outcome of a learning initiative directly to a business measure of great strategic importance.
- You will have created an opportunity for learning to help nudge the enterprise in the right direction—an opportunity that didn't exist before.

It's a great set of skills to demonstrate, one made possible by knowing every key aspect of the business, and knowing what's important to senior executives—in the language they recognize, using the terms they value.

of every CEO's most-respected information list, followed by measurements of volume, efficiency, or speed, and by any concrete evidence that the organization has been affected in a positive way. People who go out of their way to identify root causes of problems are recognized, and creative solutions that require little or no capital outlay are sure to generate positive effects. The big payoff for maintaining accountability isn't in the numbers, though; it's in the respect it generates from the top in terms of their trust and belief that those in charge of workplace learning are, among other things, making sound business decisions.

What Motivates *Your* CEO?

When communicating with a top-level executive, you are quite often dealing with someone who has a highly developed individual personality and who is quite particular about the way he or she wants the organization to work. You play by his or her rules, or you don't play at all.

Unfortunately, CEOs don't come with an instruction manual. It is helpful to understand their psychological makeup, which dictates the ways in which they are predisposed to receive and process information.

DiSC Profiling

One useful technique for characterizing people's basic psychological makeup is the DiSC profiling system which is based on the work of psychologist William Moulton Marston (1928) and refined by Michael O'Connor (Alessandra & O'Connor, 2006) (see figure 6-1). DiSC is an acronym that represents the four basic psychological types: *D* (dominance), *I* (influence), *S* (steadiness), and *C* (conscientiousness):

■ *In general,* D *(dominance) types are outgoing, decisive, take-charge people who thrive on competition.* It's not surprising that many CEOs, presidents, and top leaders are *D*-dominant personalities; it's the closest thing there is to a universal psychological component of top executives. Because they like speed and value quickness of mind, *D*-types don't want to get bogged down in lengthy, emotional discussions or hear every

The CEO Effect

CEOs come in many different guises. There are hard-charging, charismatic CEOs such as Jack Welch (ex-GE), Steve Jobs (Apple), and Richard Branson (Virgin), who court celebrity and rule their fiefdoms with autocratic zeal. There are mild-mannered but tough CEOs such as Brad Anderson (Best Buy) and Mark Hurd (HP), who lean on a close inner circle to execute their vision and are focused primarily on strategy and execution. And, there are almost-anonymous CEOs such as Darwin Smith (ex-Kimberly Clark), Colman Mockler (ex-Gillette), and David Bernauer (Walgreen's), whose companies have performed spectacularly under their leadership, but whose personal style does not put them in front of a television camera very often. Each one leads in his or her own way, and each organization reflects, to a greater or lesser degree, the personality and character of its leader.

detail behind every decision. The *D* personality type manifests itself in many different ways depending on how it is mixed with the other three basic factors of personality.

■ *I (influence) types are outgoing, people-oriented, and idealistic.* They are the sort of people who like to talk, tell jokes, and stories, and seem able to strike up a conversation with anyone. *I* people gravitate toward careers that involve working with many people, which is why so many salespeople, trainers, teachers, and public speakers are strongly in the *I* camp. In general, *I* types want to feel good about themselves and what they are doing, so they don't like to hear bad news, and they particularly don't want it mixed with a bunch of endless detail. Getting to the point and keeping it positive are the keys to crafting messages these folks want to hear.

■ *S (steadiness) types aren't very outgoing, but they are still people oriented.* They tend to have a high emotional quotient (EQ) and are sensitive to the needs and feelings of those around them. Leaders who are strong *S* types tend to be the sort who are beloved by everyone and wear their concern for their employees' well-being on their sleeve. They are kind, compassionate, reasonable people who are not given to great emotional vicissitudes. The *S* could also stand for "service," because these are the types of leaders who make a mission out of serving the customer. An *S*-dominant leader will likely be most interested in how he or she can help you, not how you can help him or her. From the CEO's chair, *S* types respond most favorably to solutions that are mutually beneficial and that serve as many people as possible as compassionately as possible. *S* leaders want people to do their jobs, but they also care that people feel good about their work and their relationship with the company.

■ C *(conscientious) types are reserved, task- and detail-oriented, and they approach work with the logical detachment of Mr. Spock of "Star Trek" fame.* Accountants, auditors, and analysts are often *C* types, as are many chief financial officers. *C* people insist on seeing numbers, they tend to regard anything that can't be counted or measured as irrelevant, and they will take as long as they need to get the information they want. Unlike *I* types, *C* folks want all the nitty-gritty details, and they want to go over the numbers line by line. When presenting to them, bring plenty of charts, graphs, and statistics, and be prepared to discuss every aspect of them in depth. Also, note that if you aren't prepared, and you can't speak knowledgeably about numbers under discussion, *C* types will not regard you as a serious person. Privately, they may even question your professional credentials. Indeed, the most difficult type of CEO to present to is someone who is *D* and *C* in equal measures. Such leaders want as much information as you can possibly give them, they want it as fast as possible, and they are intolerant of people who can't deliver the goods on both counts. The best strategy

Figure 6-1. DiSC personality profiling—a model of human behavior.

Source: Used with permission of Personality Insights, Atlanta.

for presenting to this type of leader is to be exquisitely pre-pared and know the business backward and forward. *C* types give bonus points to people who can impress them with their knowledge and skill and can also demonstrate that they've thought ahead and have already put together a detailed, step-by-step plan for accomplishing things in the future. If you can think of something they haven't and have already figured out how to deal with it, you are gold in their eyes!

Most people do not fall squarely in one category or another; they exhibit a mix of personality preferences, with one usually being more dominant than the others. It's important to understand these psycho-logical preferences because not all people want information presented to them in the same way (*Presenting With Style,* Rohm & Jeary, 2006). If your CEO is a gregarious *I* type who would rather hear the story behind the statistics than go over the numbers themselves, you might severely test his or her patience if you spend too much time crunching numbers with them. On the other hand, if your CEO is a number-and-detail *C* type, efforts to introduce levity or get too touchy-feely might be frowned upon.

Political Mapping

In the real world, one rarely makes a presentation to a CEO one-on-one. Usually others are present, too, perhaps other executives, vice presidents, managers, and so forth, each with a stake in the matter, and each with biases and a personality. Aside from their DiSC profiles, other factors may be at work behind the scenes, shaping their collective response to a presentation. Among the possibilities are ideological differences, turf battles, personal issues, disagreements over strategy and resources, or other issues that could skew the energy in the room one way or another. All are part of the politics of management, and they can play an important role in determining the success or failure of any given proposal.

The effect of such factors is difficult to predict, but part of a presenter's job is to anticipate what sort of land mines might be encountered in any given situation. Gut feelings play a large role as does institutional knowledge about the players themselves. There are more systematic ways of analyzing the presentation challenges posed by decision makers who have different areas of interest, expertise, and concern. One good way is to generate a political map of the constituents involved. This method is particularly useful when dealing with highly emotional or controversial issues because it provides a structured way of analyzing the dynamics in a given group. By knowing ahead of time which people will support your agenda and why, you will be in a better position to build a supportive alliance before a presentation, tailor your material appropriately, and leverage the existing support in the room during the presentation itself.

To start a political map, first write down the names of people or departments that have a stake in the matter at hand or have a strong opinion about it. Then, assess how much influence each person has on the issue and determine whom you need to persuade to get on board, as well as any other factors that need to be addressed. Consider both the individual's power and rank in the decision-making process and the amount of influence the person may have in the discussion.

Next, write down what you know about the individual's position on the subject or issue. A basic analysis might just note whether the person is in favor of what you are proposing. A more in-depth analysis might flesh out the personal dynamics at work or cite such organizational issues as turf wars, redundancy issues, fear of change, disagreements over strategy, and so forth. Go down the list name by name, and ask yourself the hardest questions you can think of. Is his influence so strong that he could derail the initiative altogether? Does she have a competing agenda that she's trying to protect? Try to distill an individual's support or lack of it down to the core issue that drives him or her (as opposed to the surface objection he or she may be raising.)

In the next column, write down the implications or consequences of every person's position/influence *if you did nothing before meeting with them.* In the bottom left-hand corner put a "+" to indicate support, a "−" to indicate resistance, or a "?" to indicate neutrality. In the final column, write down the actions you need to take to ensure the support of the "+"s, minimize the impact of the "−"s, and move the neutrals into the "+" category.

Figure 6-2 is a map about a hypothetical learning initiative involving some intensive sales training that would require everyone involved in sales to participate. The idea did not come from the vice president of sales, however; it came from the line managers who are battling in the trenches, who happen to see the vice president of sales as an obstacle

"I approach HR and communications with a strategic business mindset. It's difficult to work on my team unless you understand strategy and the business initiative tie-in. You must have the will to learn and grow. You can't work on my team unless you have the will to win. If you have the will, but not all of the skill, I can still work with you to improve. But if you don't have the will, it becomes more difficult to inspire and push nonmotivated people each day."

—Jeff Reeves, executive vice president, chief human resources officer, Allianz of America, and former professional football player

Figure 6-2. Example of political mapping.

Position	Person	Power/ Influence	Probable DiSC Personality Type	Position/Issue	Implication	Action
CEO	Franco	High	D	Supportive but not happy about timing	Chance of support slipping +	Address timing issue somehow
Chief operating officer	Chris	Medium	I	No big stake; can be persuaded	Support likely, but not guaranteed ?	Take temperature in advance
Chief financial officer	Sheryl	High (has veto power)	S	Needs to see the business case	Budgets are tight; case needs to be solid –	Meet to find out exactly what she wants and needs
Vice president of marketing	Loren	Low (marketing not affected)	C	No strong opinion either way	Can pick up support, for what it's worth ?	See in advance just to make sure
Vice president of sales	Trang	High (doesn't like the idea)	I	Afraid training will take too many people out of the field for too long	Will probably try to derail the whole thing or table it at the very least; key player –	Meet in advance (lunch, maybe) to discuss pros and cons; get him thinking that it's partly his idea, and that he'll get credit for its success

rather than an asset. Because the idea didn't come from the vice president of sales, he is dead set against it and sees the whole program as a sign of personal failure. Your job, as CLO, is to persuade everyone that the initiative is the right thing to do for the enterprise.

Once you've mapped the situation, it's easy to see that the vice president of sales and the chief financial officer are the ones with "–," so these represent the largest obstacles and are going to be the most critical people to persuade. With a little extra effort, it looks as if the chief operating officer and the vice president of marketing can be brought on board and that the support of the CEO can be solidified as well. If this group has the power to decide what flies and what doesn't, your job is going to be much easier if you take the time, *before meeting with them as a group,* to find out what their individual concerns are and how you can work together to resolve them.

Note that, in general, it's much more persuasive to make a case that's less about individual preferences and more about working together to do what's best for the organization. Among other things, depersonalizing conflict diminishes the amount of influence an individual is likely to have. If there are genuine differences of opinion, depersonalizing business matters also makes it possible to have constructive disagreements on some issues and still work productively together in other areas.

Make the Unknowns Known

Presentation Masters make every effort to know precisely where everyone stands *before* going into a presentation. They don't want surprises, and they want to do everything they can to ensure that the outcome they desire is going to be achieved. Presentation Masters do this by making as many of the *unknowns known* as possible, including using personality profiling to help decide how information ought to be presented and by using such techniques as political mapping to anticipate obstacles and clear them away before can do any damage.

Obviously, these techniques aren't just useful in determining what senior executives are thinking and how best to address them. They can be used to prepare for almost any type of presentation situation. For example, if you are giving a presentation to a group of engineers in the research and development department, you can be fairly certain that the room is going to be filled with lots of *C*-type personalities who want detailed information and comprehensive data, as well as *I* types who will respond more favorably to logical arguments than to emotional appeals. A group of salespeople will have an entirely different dynamic, however, and your material should be adapted accordingly.

A Presentation Puzzle

Perhaps the most difficult presentation situation for learning professionals happens when presenting to a panel of people who all have different tendencies. Maybe the CEO is a friendly *I* type, but the chief financial officer is a tough-as-nails numbers person, and the chief operating officer is an *S* type with a little *D* thrown in for the sake of authority. In such cases, one must be prepared to present the same information in several different ways. For the CEO, one must be prepared to distill information concisely; for the chief financial officer, one must be prepared to elaborate on the same information in as much depth as possible; and for the chief operating officer, one must be prepared not only to talk about numbers, but also about what those numbers mean in terms of how the organization is functioning, how effective the management structure has been at executing, and perhaps dozens of other human factors that the others might not be so interested in.

Just Do It

Personality profiling and political mapping are not difficult things to do. What separates Presentation Masters from the rest of the crowd is that they take the time to *actually do them*. You'd be surprised how clear a picture you can get of an individual or group by having the discipline to analyze their psychological characteristics in a structured way that's easy to refer to as you build your presentation strategy. Politics in any organization can be a complex puzzle. It doesn't matter what level of an organization you're working at. Whether you're a highly influential CLO, a line trainer, or an outside consultant trying to sell the value of your services to an organization, doing DiSC profiles of all the important decision makers can give you enormous insights into how to work more effectively for them and how you should interact with them when you have the opportunity. Likewise, political mapping can pay huge communication dividends, especially if you are dealing with the same people repeatedly. As you learn more about people, you can add to their profiles and eventually create what amounts to an organizational influence guidebook. Besides, writing the dynamics down in even the simplest political map can help free your mind to focus on other vital aspects of preparation.

As you grow more proficient at these methods and begin to internalize them as an everyday part of your work, the benefits will show in terms of the confidence you are able to bring to your job, and the results you are eventually able to achieve. Knowing with whom you're dealing and how to deal with them are a Presentation Master's two most valuable assets. Don't go into a presentation without them.

Are You the CEO's Right Hand?

The old ways of structuring power (hierarchies, bureaucracy, seniority, control) are dying. Leaders today are embracing new ideas that put a premium on flexibility, transparency, empowerment, networks, collaboration, mentoring, and knowledge. According to Christopher Bartlett and Sumantra Ghoshal (2002, p. xi), "Today's managers are trying to implement third-generation strategies through second-generation organizations with first-generation management." What they mean is that the ideas shaping our social systems and institutions are moving faster than the institutions themselves and the people running them.

Many CEOs today were trained to be analytical directors of organizational strategy and financial resources, they say, not people-oriented framers of culture and vision. Former GE chief Jack Welch once remarked that "a company's value lies between the ears of its employees." Today's CEOs are having to learn the people part of the job on the fly, which means that you, the resident expert on people and their performance, are the perfect person to help them—and help them you must.

Very Important Points

- To understand how CEOs think, presenters of learning need to understand them both as individuals and in the context of the larger enterprise they are running.

- Remember that CEOs want metrics and data because they help explain what is going on in the company to the people who are judging *their* performance—board members and shareholders.

- If you want to understand what a CEO's motivations are, find out how his or her performance is being measured and what incentive targets he or she is being required to meet.

- Learning professionals need to develop keen business minds and business-oriented professional practices. This means learning and comprehending the language of finance, even if it means taking a course to do it. It also means operating with the same rules of discipline and accountability as other key departments.

- Use the DiSC profiling system to determine what the prevailing psychologies of your senior executives are and then present information to them in ways their mindset prefers.

- Use political mapping to understand the power dynamics at work in the organization and to anticipate obstacles that may prevent you from achieving your objectives.

- If you want to be a Presentation Master, make every effort to know where everyone stands *before* going into a presentation so that there are no surprises and you can be reasonably sure of the outcome in advance.

In this chapter, you took a closer look at some of your most important audiences—your CEO and other senior executives—and learned what makes them tick. Armed with this insight, you'll be ready to tackle the next chapter in which you will learn more about using the language of business to build a case for learning.

Making a Business Case
for Learning

To the Point

Learning professionals often face the task of having to build a solid business case for whatever they are proposing. This needn't be a gut-wrenching chore. In this chapter, we've put together some guidelines for how to build a business case, what sort of information is expected from upper executives, and how best to present it. We've also provided a presentation checklist for evaluating the cases you put together, as well as some strategies for discussing benefits of workplace learning that aren't always visible on a spreadsheet.

M uch of the reason why learning professionals are so preoccupied with trying to use various evaluations and assessments for training effectiveness is to help develop a solid business rationale for learning's existence. The fear is that without such a rationale, learning's true value will go unrecognized by the organization's senior executives, and it will become a meaty target the next time budgets need to be trimmed.

Whether you're talking about a project or a tiered initiative, the best offense against such a fate is to build a solid business case for whatever learning you are proposing. Some learning professionals bristle at the idea of having to play by business's rules, but if you do it well, those rules will work in your favor. When presenting the business case for learning, some up-front expectations need to be met, a few predictable questions need to be answered, and a certain protocol should be followed for presenting the information. But, when you break it down, the requirements of a solid business case aren't as demanding as you might think.

What Is a Business Case Anyway?

Making a business case means coming up with clear, concise, logical reasons why something should be done—reasons that connect the hoped-for results of the action with the mission and goals of the organization. In the strictest sense, everything that happens in a business should be supported or motivated by a strong business rationale, and if something doesn't make business sense, it probably shouldn't be done. Learning gets caught in the cracks because no one has yet devised a simple, easy-to-understand, tried-and-true method for proving that learning solution A caused events B, C, and D to happen. In a leadership seminar for 10 managers, two of them might go on to be company superstars, four might ignore the training and exhibit no change in their managing skills whatsoever, two might try a few things but get mixed results, and two might figure out some creative way to use the training to become worse managers than they were before. When the CEO asks whether this seminar "worked," that is, did it achieve any tangible results (beyond the fact that everyone had fun and really enjoyed the program) that they can see, the true answer would be yes, maybe, probably not, and no. That's not the sort of answer a business-minded executive wants to hear. Unfortunately, learning professionals often rely on metrics such as reaction and knowledge transfer that, while important, are disconnected from the information that the executive is seeking.

To help learning professionals get past this obstacle, we've put together some guidelines about what is expected when presenting a business case for learning and the basic flow such presentations should have. There is more than one way to build a business case, of course, but a strong business case, whatever the subject or proposal, is generally built by following 11 basic steps, outlined in the sections that follow.

Step 1: Identify the Decision Makers and Stakeholders

Whether you are an internal employee or an outside consultant, if you are going to present learning effectively, you need to know who is going to make the final decision on approval and you need to know who else has an interest or stake in the decision. If you are part of an internal learning department, the chain of command may be clear and your role depends on where you are located in that chain. The higher up the chain you are, the closer you are to the final decision makers and the more power you have to influence the outcome.

It's a little trickier if you are coming at it from the outside because you may not always be aware of all the internal politics or the informal power structures that are part of every organization. In some ways, coming at it from the outside can be easier, though, because if you are an executive coach, say, you will have been brought in for a specific reason with specific measures, and you may be working directly with one or two people. To be sure, many outside vendors prefer to bypass the HR and training departments altogether to avoid getting bogged down by bureaucracy and turf wars.

In any event, as you build your business case, you always need to keep in mind who your audience is going to be, what they want to hear, and how they want to hear it. Knowing whom you have to persuade in the end will help guide your thinking as you gather information and develop your case. This is where political mapping (discussed in the preceding chapter) can be extremely helpful. In particular, you should note people who have veto power or could otherwise derail your initiative and people whose support would grease the wheels of acceptance. It's also helpful, over time, to develop personal friendships and connections with decision makers as part of the trust-building process. The more comfortable decision makers are with you, both personally and professionally, the less effort you have to expend establishing your own credibility.

Step 2: Listen to Stakeholders' Needs

In the past, training was thought of primarily as a utilitarian business function, and listening to management's needs amounted to little more than picking up the phone and taking orders. Various departments in an organization basically told learning departments what sort of training they needed, and the sole job of the training department was to provide the requested courses of instruction.

In the emerging proactive business-partner paradigm of learning, however, such phone calls are becoming rarer. That's because part of the learning department's mission is to go out and engage key stakeholders about their problems and issues *before* anyone has made a decision about what type of training, if any, is needed. Members of the department essentially play the role of a consultant, one who does a great deal of due diligence to find out what the organization's challenges are and who, having gathered and digested this information, is willing to speak the truth to the powers that be about the most effective ways to meet those challenges.

To listen constructively, learning professionals need to go into discussions with an open mind. People cannot listen effectively if they have a pet training course they want to implement and are simply listening for ways to slap their favorite solution onto a problem. The listening has to be focused on the needs of the organization and how learning can most effectively address those needs.

Besides listening for what learning can do, you should also be listening for things learning can't or shouldn't do. That is, you should be listening for mistaken assumptions or expectations about training's ability

Discovering CSC's Needs

Computer Sciences Corporation's CLO Holly Huntley spends months deploying her team on pulse-taking missions throughout the company. She pools the information from those interviews with information gathered from various skills and competency tests and then creates her own call plan to visit all the relevant stakeholders and discuss the problems uncovered and solutions that are being developed, securing buy-in and consensus along the way.

"You have to anticipate what the needs of executives are before they figure it out themselves," Huntley advises. "Ultimately, my goal is to make them look good. So, I do a lot of environmental scanning to bring them solutions in a proactive way. If I bring up a problem, I bring the solution, too."

to solve certain problems because they may not be training issues at all. For example, if a sales manager's team isn't performing up to speed, his reflexive conclusion might be that the troops should be put through some intensive sales training to learn how to answer objections better and achieve a higher close rate. But, what if after discussing the issue of lagging sales with the actual salespeople and other related constituents it's discovered that the real problem has to do with a lack of sufficient product knowledge, or anger over the management style of the manager himself, or a bad incentive system, or a lack of product support that is alienating customers and sending them to the competition?

Each of *those* problems requires a different solution. But, if you had simply taken the manager at his word, you would have supplied him with the requested sales training program, which would have satisfied the manager's theoretical needs of the moment but would have done little or nothing to solve his problem. After giving his sales team "the training," the manager's natural expectations would be that he would see a measurable jump in sales. When that failed to happen, he might come to the conclusion that "training doesn't work," and end up being a voice of dissent or skepticism when future training initiatives are considered.

Such shortsighted cycles of ignorance don't help anyone. They make training look bad, they disappoint people, they generate resistance to other initiatives in the future, and they don't help the organization move forward. The fact is, though, that throwing well-meaning but unhelpful or ill-conceived training programs at misdiagnosed or misunderstood problems is *how things have been done for decades!* It's ridiculous, really. And the workplace learning profession is addressing this issue with the practice of human performance improvement.

After all, what would you think of a doctor who allows the patient to tell him or her what course of treatment they needed and then just gave it to them? Or a golf instructor who simply lets people swing a club however they like? Or a psychiatrist who accepts every patient's story at face value? You would think they were incompetent. You would think they have no idea what they are doing. You would think they are trying to trick you. And, if you happened to *be* that doctor, golf instructor, or psychiatrist, you would be doing your customers or patients a great disservice. You might even be guilty of criminal negligence.

Step 3: Define Success

Being proactive, having a deep understanding of the business, and listening intently to determine what people's true needs are won't eliminate all the sources of error in communication between learning professionals and their constituents, but it's a good initial step. For those who struggle with measurement issues or who battle the perception that training does not work as well as expected, identifying the criteria for success is an extremely important step. Defining success—and thereby managing expectations about what success will look like—is crucial because it is the benchmark against which your efforts will be judged. If the bar is set too high, if expectations are unrealistic, everyone is going to be disappointed. And, if you, the learning professional, allow it to happen by promising too much, believing too enthusiastically in a program, or by not adequately vetting its actual benefits, you're just undermining your own cause by making promises you can't keep.

Another psychological paradox of training is at work here as well. The temptation for many who believe passionately in the power of learning is to think of it as something from which everyone can benefit or as a cure-all that can fix all organizational ills. But, in practice, there are limitations to what training can realistically accomplish. Some people get more out of training than others and some do more with the training they receive than others.

Consider the previous example involving the 10 managers and multiple outcomes. If your expectation is that the training will affect all the managers equally and that they should all demonstrate a level of performance improvement to some extent, you are going to be disappointed to discover that this didn't happen. But, what if one of the stated goals of the training was simply to identify high performers—to weed out the bottom 90 percent and flush out your superstars? In that case, you would be happy to discover that the training did exactly what you had hoped: it identified two people in the group of 10 as outstanding potential leaders.

Top executives tend to look at problems and ask such questions as: "Is this the best we can do? How can we improve our performance? Why isn't X resulting in Y?" You have to be very careful about how you answer those questions, though, because you don't want to get trapped promising something you can't deliver. The key is to get *them* to tell *you* what their hopes and expectations are so that you can negotiate reasonable, agreed-upon targets and benchmarks. Among the questions that need to be asked are the following:

- Is training the best way to solve the problem? (It may not be.)
- What are the desired results?
- How do those results connect with specific strategic objectives?
- Are the results measurable, and can they be isolated to a single individual or group?
- If so, what should be measured, and what tools or processes should be used to measure or recognize results?

- If it is not possible to isolate the impact of the learning solution, what is the agreed-upon impact of that solution? (Preferably, this number will come from the recipients of learning.)

- If the necessary measurement tools and processes aren't in place, is the organization willing to invest in them?

- If the organization is not willing to invest in measurement instruments, what behavioral changes or comparative analyses would suffice as adequate substitutes?

- Are there valuable intangibles involved that would benefit the organization but currently are being overlooked?

- What happens if the initial goals aren't met? Will there be an opportunity for follow-up and continued increase in improvement?

Once the criteria for success are established, deciding realistic targets and benchmarks becomes much easier and the likelihood of reaching them and delivering on the promise of the learning rises dramatically.

Step 4: Create a Compelling Context

Every leadership decision is made in a context of fluid forces and events, and it is a leader's job to filter through this flood of information and make sense of it so that smart decisions can be made. Likewise, learning initiatives are never presented in a vacuum; they occur in a dynamic world of shifting influences and business factors. One of the great things about presentations is that they give the presenter the opportunity to define his or her own context for the information he or she is present-ing—and it is an opportunity no presenter should pass up.

Creating the context for the story you are going to tell is much like gathering background research for a novel. Your goal is to find informa-tion that is not only relevant to the situation you are discussing, but also frames your initiative in a favorable light or sheds fresh insight into the challenges facing the organization and how you plan to address them.

Trends. Senior management is not likely to be up to speed on the latest trends in learning, so it's the learning professional's job to bring this information to them but only in selective slices. Look for relevant articles from reputable sources such as the *Harvard Business Review* and the *Wall Street Journal,* and in industry magazines such as *T+D, Training,* and *CLO.* Gather background data, demographic information, and other statistics from industry and government websites, reports, blogs, white papers—anything that will objectively validate what you're saying. The purpose of gathering such information is to enhance your credibility as an expert and to help make your arguments more persuasive. It's much more convincing to say, "According to the U.S. Department of Labor and Statistics, in five years there will be 10 million more jobs in the United States than there are people to fill them," than to say, "In five years, I have a hunch talent will be scarce."

Or, rather than just coming out and saying, "We need better succession planning," preceding it with something like: "The Saratoga Institute conducted more than 19,000 exit interviews of key employees leaving companies and found that 80 percent said they left due to poor management and leadership or because of a dysfunctional company culture. However, 85 percent of bosses thought their top people left for more money and opportunity." Opinions are OK, but opinions backed up by facts are compelling!

Best Practices. Comparing the organization's practices and capabilities with those of better-performing companies or close competitors is another way to frame learning discussions. Presentation Masters keep files full of best-practice information and are continually feeding and updating those files to keep them current. Why? Because if a close competitor is doing something you would like to try, it's much more persuasive to say something like, "Company XYZ has implemented a similar program and has seen a 7 percent rise in productivity, whereas 3 percent is the best we have been able to do. I think we can do better, and here's how." It's almost impossible for top executives to ignore what the competition is doing, so use that preoccupation to your advantage when you can.

Keeping up on best practices, as a matter of principle, is also one of the best ways to ensure that your organization stays competitive. They are a great source of new ideas and if your research is diligent and consistent enough, just knowing about them gives you a competitive advantage. Not only does it communicate to those in the organization that you are plugged into the right information channels, it says that your priorities are in the right place and that quality and excellence are your guiding values.

Track Records. Everyone has a history of successes and failures that add up to one word: *experience.* Any time you can draw on a past personal success to illustrate prospects for the future, you are demonstrating the value and applicability of your experience. Not only does it reinforce your credibility and remind people that you have an established record of success, but also it indicates that you are capable of delivering success in the future. This is important because most executives are less interested in what happened yesterday than what is going to happen tomorrow. The future is where the great beast of uncertainty lies, and a record of success goes a long way toward reassuring skeptical executives that you can get the job done. Even failures can work to your advantage in this area, providing you learned something important from the experience and can demonstrate how this knowledge has prepared you for the challenge ahead.

Organizations have track records, too, and one advantage of having a deep knowledge of an organization is knowing where the skeletons and landmines are hidden so that you don't repeat the same mistakes. Senior executives have long memories, so being able to refer to previous failures or disappointments is often a powerful tactic to use if you are confident that your solution can turn things around or eliminate the concern altogether.

Obstacles and Roadblocks. Knowledge of what has worked in the past and what hasn't also gives you a better, more holistic appreciation for the systemic issues that might crop up at any given time. One of the best ways to create value as a business partner is to anticipate and neutralize problems before they happen. When presenting your ideas, be candid about obstacles and roadblocks but also show how you propose to get around them.

If you don't have an immediate solution, it's still better to share your concerns than to hide them. If you hide information, it may come back to haunt you in any number of ways. If you share it, you communicate that you are not afraid to talk about concerns that are beyond your power to control. Sometimes, being humble in the face of adversity is the best option.

Timeframes and Expectations. Managing expectations for learning initiatives is an extremely important part of the presentation or negotiation process. One good way to break down expectations is to establish a timeline for certain results to take root and spread. After a leadership development seminar, for instance, it is unrealistic to expect everyone to suddenly go out the following day and demonstrate spectacular leadership skills. Over the course of a month or two, however, you might begin to see some behavior shifts that are having some effects. Maybe meetings are shorter or managers have figured out how to deal more effectively with problem employees or they are managing their time better. After a quarter, you might see leadership demonstrated in tangible ways, such as someone taking on a project he or she might otherwise have passed on a few months before. In six months to a year, you might be able to see a pattern of decision making that suggests the growth of greater confidence and business acumen.

The point is that if you allow people to expect immediate results right out of the gate when you know that it isn't going to happen, you are setting yourself up for failure and setting your superiors up for disappointment. You owe it to yourself and the organization to be as candid as possible about what a program can and cannot achieve in a given timeframe. Benchmark and measure things as much as you want, but make sure your timeframes are realistic.

Keep in mind also that economic returns from most programs are not instantaneous. Indeed, one of the reasons knowledge derived from learning is so difficult to track is that it multiplies in unpredictable ways as it spreads via shared work experiences, casual conversations, meetings, email, and all the other ways information is spread in a vibrant organization. Some estimates are that up to 80 percent of learning on the job happens as a result of people leaning over and asking the person in the next cube how to solve a problem. It takes time for that knowledge multiplier to kick in, so it's more constructive to get people thinking of learning as something that spreads benefits in widening circles of influence rather than something that delivers immediate, tangible results to the bottom line. It's wise to counsel patience when the situation requires it.

Metrics. These days, selling a learning initiative is difficult to do without some concrete idea of how it is going to impact the organization. For decision makers at the top, feel-good testimonials aren't enough: You need solid results or at least the promise of solid results in the future. Metrics are how such results are quantified.

The phrase "measure what matters" is the all-purpose motto of learning consultants, but "what matters" is different for every organization. As a rule, top-level executives are interested in anything that lowers costs, drives revenue, improves efficiency (saves time), makes the organization more competitive, or adds value directly to the bottom line. All of these areas can be influenced by training; the challenge is and always has been establishing a direct correlation between something that happened in a classroom six weeks ago and a favorable uptick on a spreadsheet today. That's why it helps if you can narrow things down to a few specific metrics with realistic targets and an approved measurement process, all of which are agreed upon well before training begins. If you try to do it on the fly, or wait until afterward to figure out what you're going to measure, it will be too late.

Ideally, management tells you what matters to them, you tell them what's necessary to get the result they want, and they fund you accordingly. That's not always the way it works, though. Sometimes executives want evidence of results but don't see the need to invest the time and money necessary to get it. This often leaves learning professionals stranded at level 1 evaluations, gathering so-called "smile sheets" (individual course evaluations) and recording the number of hours employees have logged in the classroom or online. The information gathered from these exercises is of little value when determining any sort of impact or results from training. It is obligatory recordkeeping, nothing more. Executives want to understand the quantifiable link between learning and business results, so savvy professionals do what they can to provide these answers.

If you have no metrics whatsoever to work with, numbers can sometimes be borrowed from other organizations to help illustrate possibilities. In cases where adequate processes for gathering metrics aren't in place, keep pushing the case for more sophisticated tracking of data, especially as it pertains to the achievement of stated goals and objectives.

Trust. In matters of persuasion, nothing is more important than trust. Trust is built over time and usually depends on having close relationships with decision makers, as well as delivering consistently reliable results over time. If people trust you and your judgment, they may be willing to overlook shortcomings in data, questions about the viability of a program, concerns about staffing, or any number of other things that could waylay a proposal from someone less credible.

Ultimately, trust is a matter of responsibility and accountability. You must be honest in your dealings with people, do what you say you're going to do, follow through on everything, and demonstrate through your actions an unwavering commitment to the organization's goals and objectives. You must also be competent at your job, of course, but honesty and integrity are arguably more important than a flawless record of success when it comes to establishing trust. If you can put trust and competency together, however, you will find that your powers of persuasion are likely to improve dramatically.

Step 5: Establish Authority, Reliability, Credibility

The more credible and reliable you are as a person, the more likely people are to believe what you say and agree with you. Like trust, however, credibility does not happen instantaneously; it's earned over time and is a function of the results you have achieved in the past. When building a business case for learning, it's important that you have the full confidence of upper management, which means that it's often necessary to remind them why you and your team can do the job better than anyone else can. A stellar record helps, of course, but there are other ways to gain instant respect as well:

- Prove that you have done your research and thought things through. Guide them through your thought process and show them how you arrived at the solution you are proposing.

- Play devil's advocate and ask yourself the hard questions before they do.

- When you identify a problem or challenge, suggest solutions. It proves that you're looking at both sides of an issue—a key expectation of leadership.

- Play the role of change agent, and, in the interest of improving the organization, force management to face some uncomfortable truths. Executives respect courage and candor.

- Be aware of any history with your department that might cause someone to question you or the department's credibility. If such a history exists, explain why things are different now. But be careful to not appear defensive.

- Demonstrate that you are an expert in the field by using examples from competitors or other parts of the industry or by citing the work of analysts in the field.

- Draw parallels with your previous work, if you are an outside consultant trying to sell your services.

- Get testimonials from previous clients and keep them in a binder to serve as a portfolio of your achievements. Share them when appropriate.

Step 6: Connect the Program to the Organization's Mission

Upper management sometimes rejects programs because they feel wrong or don't quite feel right for the organization and its culture, so it's important to reinforce the idea that a program is a good fit. If you've done your job correctly, this should not just be an assertion on your part, it should be a fact you've already established. If not—if you just mouth the words to make people feel better about a proposal— you risk a blow to your credibility if it doesn't work out.

Likewise, a direct connection to the organization's mission and goals should not be a stretch. All learning initiatives should be backed by a clear rationale. Everyone in the organization, from the CEO on down, should be able to understand the reasons for the initiative, because the *need* for it should have arisen from specific business issues or objectives. If no connection exists or if the rationale seems fuzzy, the initiative needs to be scrapped, the impetus for it needs to be clarified, or, at a minimum, the initiative should be rethought.

Step 7: Be Flexible

In today's increasingly global, competitive, diversified workplace, there is no one-size-fits-all learning solution. To be successful, solutions need to address the specific needs of an organization. As the learning management role in organizations becomes more strategic, this also means being open to solutions that combine the proper mix of content, tools, resources, and technology in the way that addresses the problem most effectively, not necessarily the solution that suits the training management team. This means being "solution agnostic" about whether to use outside resources or to do everything in-house.

Of course, good off-the-shelf programs do exist and are useful for routine types of training, but the supplier community is also taking on more of a consulting role in working with clients. Sometimes, the best friend a learning professional can have is a reliable network of outside vendors, consultants, and executive coaches who, even though they are not technically on the payroll, act as an extended team. (See example of Sandia National Laboratories on following page.)

Sandia National Laboratories

Sandia National Laboratories (SNL) and course designers De La Porte & Associates (DLP&A) have just such a partnership. Sandia is a subsidiary of Lockheed Martin that employs 8,600 people and does $2.3 billion worth of work each year. A few years ago, SNL's business development process was in chaos, with scientists and engineers basically developing whatever they felt like, hoping that one day they would hit on a sellable product. The company needed to overhaul its business development process and the training curriculum that went with it so that the company could start identifying potential customer needs first and then create products to meet those needs.

After many conversations, consultations, and needs assessments, SNL and DLP&A set up an advanced sales training (AST) program. The program is a blend of classroom training, skills practice, and refresher activities, as one might expect, but it also includes the critical element of individual and team coaching. The coaching component is critical because the aspect of business development that SNL's technicians and engineers needed the most help with was the human side of things: personal interaction, relationship building, and assessing the true needs and desires of potential customers.

To assess the bottom-line impact of the AST program, SNL did not rely on internal reporting mechanisms. Instead, to ensure accuracy and eliminate any possible bias, it hired two outside agencies to do independent analyses. The exact results of those reports are proprietary because much of Sandia's work is with the federal government, but Kathleen Schulz, principal business development consultant at SNL, reports that the results from the program are "exponentially superior" to industry averages, which is why it continues to receive funding. According to Schulz, there is now a waiting list of people who want to enter the program. In 2005, SNL awarded DLP&A its Gold President's Quality Award, the highest honor an outside partner can achieve working with SNL.

In partnerships like the one between SNL and DLP&A, the line between internal and external becomes almost meaningless because the working relationship is so close. The only difference, really, is how the checks are processed. Otherwise, it is a complete partnership in every sense of the word. The changing nature of learning's role in enterprises, combined with the increasing sophistication and diversification of the vendor community, is making such arrangements much more common.

Step 8: Envision Success

When presenting learning, the central subject is really what the future is going to look like when the learning is implemented. Toward that end, it's the learning professional's job to guide the imaginations of executives so that they can envision the improved future in their own minds. In cases where there is a well-defined problem and an agreed-upon solution, envisioning a future with the problem removed or fixed isn't particularly difficult. But, in cases where the value is likely to be more intangible or where it may take some time to see the benefits of a program accrue, a little creative storytelling can go a long way.

■ *Help them imagine what success will look like in their terms.* Whether they're looking for higher sales, faster cycle times, improved processes, or more compelling innovation, identify the numbers that will be affected. Don't just talk about the numbers, though, talk about what the numbers *mean to them.* A 10 percent improvement in the number of customer service calls a department can handle is a good thing, but it's a much better thing if you can also point out how it will improve customer relations, make the company more competitive, generate goodwill in the user community, drive future sales, and so forth. Connect the numbers with the real-world processes that create those numbers, and paint a picture in their minds of how success will look when it is achieved.

◼ *Expand the organizational impact.* One big advantage of knowing how the organization operates is that you can extrapolate benefits beyond the immediate rewards of a program. A program may only involve 30 people, but those 30 people might go out and interact with 300 other people, spreading what they've learned in all kinds of ways. For example, a faster and more customer-friendly way of checking out groceries might save time and make customers happier, but if it's sufficiently innovative, it could pull business from competitors, generate positive media coverage, and enhance the overall perception of the brand in the community. Learning events aren't isolated; they ripple throughout the organization in both predictable and unpredictable ways and often yield benefits that are overlooked. Talking about such ancillary benefits also reinforces the idea that learning is an integral and inextricable part of an organization's success, a part that can't simply be downsized or eliminated without serious consequences.

◼ *Explain what the consequences might be if the training doesn't happen.* If you can't identify specific, concrete ways in which a program will benefit the organization, try explaining what will happen if the training doesn't happen at all. Otherwise known as the "can it get any worse?" approach, assuming a negative can sometimes imply a positive. "I can't promise you that things are going to improve, but if we don't try to change, I can assure you that things won't improve and will likely get worse." Delays, inefficiencies, mistakes, rework, lost customers, quality slippage, brand deterioration, productivity declines, morale, employee and customer loyalty—all of these things have a value associated with them and all can affect an organization negatively if they are not managed correctly. Everyone knows this, which is why the threat of bad things happening if some sort of action isn't taken can be such a powerful tool of persuasion, albeit one that should be used sparingly.

■ *Note what the competition is doing.* Often, pointing out what the competition is doing will spur action when other tactics won't. The more detail you have on the competition's activities, the better. If you can demonstrate that what the competition is doing represents a competitive threat of some sort or makes the organization look bad or negligent in some way, you will have everyone's attention.

■ *Present best-case and worst-case scenarios.* Executives know that results are never guaranteed, so they often like to hear things framed in a best-case/worst-case format. Whenever you frame the discussion this way, however, always be able to estimate the likelihood of success and back up your assessment with solid reasoning.

Step 9: Cultivate Cheerleaders and Champions

Part of building an effective consensus is also identifying and developing cheerleaders and champions. Cheerleaders are people who enthusiastically support what you are doing and will back you up when asked. Champions are people who support you and are excited by your plans and who also have the power to help you implement them.

Champions and cheerleaders are best identified during the proactive listening phase, when people in the organization are being asked about their learning needs and they know you are there to help them. As you talk to people, keep a list of who supports you and how strong their support is. To secure loyalty during crunch time, come right out and say, "This program we're talking about could run into some resistance. Can I count on your support if things get dicey?"

Champions are especially important to develop, and the higher up the organization, the better. It goes without saying that if you have the support of the president or CEO, the road to adoption is going to be much smoother. Securing the backing of people who have influence with the top decision makers can be just as effective, though, especially if you are an outside consultant trying to convince an organization that you have the solution it needs.

One of the best ways to cultivate champions high in the power structure is to show how your initiative will reflect positively on the organization and, by association, them as well. Tell them how it will improve their department's profile in the organization; how it will improve the profitability of their business unit; how it will establish them as forward-thinking mavericks; how it will make them look like a champion of innovation, not a slave to the status quo. Use your Presentation Mastery skills to persuade but be absolutely certain that your initiative actually can do what you claim it can.

The bottom line is that it pays to go into any type of persuasive negotiation with as much support on your side as possible. Presentation Masters constantly send out feelers to see how and what people are thinking. If they are shopping a proposal around, they continually seek feedback, partly to improve the proposal itself, but also to get an idea of who is responding positively and who isn't. Email is a great tool for briefly touching base with people and taking their temperature. If you need more people on your side, those who are sitting on the fence can usually be persuaded with a brief personal interaction. In general, people like to help other people, so if you just come out and ask them for their support, they'll usually give it to you if it's something they don't feel strongly about either way.

Step 10: Have a Backup Plan

Training is expensive, so expensive that most large organizations don't even know how much they spend in total on it. Still, management teams are paid to be prudent, so chances are that even if management likes your proposal and supports the direction you're going, they are going to ask if you can somehow get the same results for less money. If you say no, they may accept your answer and give you what you want, or they may demand that you figure out a way to get the same results for less money.

Because budget compromises are an institutional certainty in many organizations, it's wise to prepare at least two different budgets, one for show and a pared-down one you can keep in your back pocket just in case. Don't share your Plan B unless you have to but definitely have a Plan B in place. Among other things, having a backup plan can give you a booster shot of confidence when it comes time to negotiate. Knowing that you're not married to a particular proposal can take some of the pressure off and gives you greater control over the eventual outcome. If a budget compromise is necessary, you will have already thought the implications through and will be in a more favorable position to negotiate a better deal.

Step 11: Stress Accountability

If you are serious about making the business case for learning, you must also be serious about delivering results and being accountable for both successes and failures. The best way to demonstrate your sincerity in this area is to insist that certain targets and benchmarks be established, personally guarantee that mutually agreed-upon milestones will be achieved in a given period, closely monitor the measuring process to make sure it's professional and accurate, and do everything within the budget to which you have agreed. Upper executives respect people who take personal responsibility for everything they do and don't come to the table with a list of excuses why things didn't happen the way they were supposed to or aren't going to happen the way management envisions. Results are what matter most to decision makers, and if you can't deliver results, the least you can do is accept responsibility, communicate early and often that the agreed-upon results are in jeopardy, and demonstrate an understanding of why the results weren't achieved and how this understanding will guide you in the future.

Weaving It All Together Into a Business Case

There is no one right way to put a compelling business case together. What works for one person in one organization might not work for another person in another organization. Nevertheless, you can draw upon some general rules as you are building a business case for learning, and it does help if you remember that this process isn't much different from crafting a persuasive argument in any profession. Table 7-1 presents a checklist of things you should consider as you construct a business case for learning.

What If You Can't Show Them the Money?

Although presenting a business case often boils down to dollars and cents, sometimes that's just not possible. The numbers aren't there. You can't promise anything. Revenue isn't involved. Maybe it's a seminar to manage charitable giving, or a yoga class to relieve stress, or an inspirational speaker who does nothing but—inspire. Whatever it is, if you can't make a solid business case for it, the best thing to do is to be honest about that fact up front. In such situations, you must manage expectations well enough to deflect questions about the bottom line and shift the conversation to benefits and outcomes, however intangible they may be.

It helps to remember that most senior executives, even the most budget-conscious ones, want the same things as everyone else. They want their people to be happy and inspired in their work. They want to create an environment in which everyone is working up to their capabilities and growing into new ones. They want employees to be proud of their organization and its management. They also want the learning function of the organization, whether it's one person or a battalion of staff and consultants, to help create the dynamic culture they desire.

To be sure, learning professionals must remain engaged in discussions with management about the relationship between an organization's learning function and its culture. Everyone agrees on the benefits of a healthy culture, but not everyone understands what goes into creating a great organizational culture. In the knowledge economy, learning is playing an increasingly important role in the development of people's skills and capabilities, and it is vital in the race to keep pace with the acceleration of information transfer that is now possible through ever-improving technologies and infrastructure. Decision makers worth their

Table 7-1. The business case for learning checklist.

Use this checklist to help you prepare. Do you have:

☐ A clear understanding of your audience and its needs

☐ A story or theme that ties the elements of your presentation together

☐ Learning metrics and jargon translated into the language of business

☐ A clear idea of what success looks like and the way to get there

☐ Logical connections between the stated strategy and objectives, the proposed initiative, and the desired results

☐ A context for communicating the value of the proposal through comparative statistics, competitive intelligence, industry standards and trends, best practices, anecdotal evidence, and so on

☐ Metrics for measuring results in requested areas, particularly those dealing with effectiveness, efficiency, and speed

☐ Evidence of your credibility and reliability

☐ Evidence that you've done your homework and are aware of the financial resources available to you, the business implications of anything you propose, and real-world consequences of failure

☐ Evidence that the program is a good fit for the organization's culture and values

☐ Projections about the success of the program and its potential effects on individuals and the organization

☐ A thorough explanation of how a program is going to be executed and why the chosen method or mix of methods was selected

☐ A persuasive rationale explaining why your solution is the best, most cost-effective one available

☐ Answers about resource allocation, time commitments, cost-per-learner, or any other variable affected by the program

☐ Reinforcement of the idea that the solution grew out of the organization's business needs, not out of anyone's imaginative guesses

☐ A tireless focus on and commitment to the results that top management wants to see?

salt should be taking such realities into account when they look at their organization's big picture. There should be room in that picture for things that don't directly impact the bottom line, but which everyone can agree are necessary for creating the sort of dynamic, motivated, loyal workforce that will keep the organization going for decades to come.

Ever since Donald Kirkpatrick introduced his four levels of training evaluation more than 40 years ago, trainers have been trying to deal with the business-case issue in a thoughtful, systematic way that captures the full breadth of learning's potential. Sometimes, the best approach to use, when bottom-line justification just doesn't work, is to demonstrate the benefits of learning by sharing a story or anecdote about a specific employee, a leadership challenge, or an improved business process to illustrate outcomes through narrative or metaphor.

After all, when a CEO asks, "What's the business case for the action you're proposing?" what he or she is really saying is, "Tell me a story that will convince me that what you are saying is true and that it's worth doing." Measurement data and analytics may be part of that story, but they are not the whole story. They may be able to shed some light on what happened, but they can't explain how or why it happened, whether there were good or bad unintended consequences, whether there might be a larger, more important meaning behind the numbers, or what is likely to happen in the future.

Lessons Learned: Improving Your Presentations

Although there is a great deal of work involved in building a solid business case for learning and creating content solutions that deliver the promised results, the success or failure in communication of those programs—regardless of their actual worth—often comes down to questions of how well your presentation and ongoing communications worked. If you want to improve, take some time after each presentation and ask yourself these questions:

- How thoroughly did you prepare?
- How much due diligence did you do on the people in the room?

- How well did you construct your argument?
- How well did you articulate the benefits of the proposal?
- Did you have any champions to support you?
- Were you confident when discussing your own credibility?
- Did you have sufficient data to support your claims?
- Did you demonstrate enough industry knowledge to be regarded as an expert?
- Were there aspects of your presentation that you left to chance?
- Were there holes in your argument that went unfilled?
- Did you provide credible, thorough answers to their questions?
- Did they ask questions you failed to anticipate?

Review every presentation performance as soon you can, so that it's still fresh in your mind. Be honest with yourself, and write down reminders on an index card about areas that need extra effort next time.

Very Important Points

- "Business" isn't a dirty word, and making a business case for learning isn't as difficult as it's sometimes made out to be.
- Think of making a business case as telling a story, a story in which the object is to sell an idea.
- Learn to speak the language of business, which is essentially the language of finance, results, and accountability.
- When presenting learning, it's important to craft arguments in language that executives understand and in terms they find meaningful.
- Always keep in mind who the decision makers are, what they want to hear, and how they want to hear it.
- Talk to stakeholders to find out what the organization's learning needs are, and approach each conversation with a completely open mind about what the ideal solution might be.

- Listen for expectations about learning that are unrealistic or inflated. You don't want to get trapped making promises you can't keep.

- Make sure to identify what success will look like and what criteria will be used to judge it.

- Build a compelling context for your proposals, using industry trends, best practices, and metrics that establish your expertise, build credibility, and instill trust in your judgment.

- Be sure to establish a solid connection between the organization's strategies and objectives and the results of the program you are proposing.

- Be "solution agnostic" when it comes to devising programs and content. Strive to deliver the solution that's the best for the organization, not necessarily the best for your department or you.

- Help your audience envision success by painting a vivid picture of how your proposal will affect the organization.

- Build support and negotiating power by cultivating cheerleaders and champions.

- Prepare at least two different plans, with two separate budgets, just in case.

- If you want to earn the respect of senior executives, stress accountability, responsible reporting, and economic efficiency.

Here, you learned a tremendous amount about building and presenting a business case for learning initiatives. The chapter included a couple of useful tools—a checklist for preparing your business case and a list of items to consider as you review your presentation—that will serve you well as you hone your Presentation Mastery effectiveness. In the next chapter, you'll learn more about how to make that critical link between organizational strategies and learning methodologies and outcomes.

8

Measuring Value: A Balanced Look at Scorecards

To the Point

Learning professionals often are trapped by the expectation that they can somehow figure out a way to deliver high-level reporting, results, and alignment with low-level measurement methods and inadequate resources. Making meaningful measurements an integral part of the planning process is essential. Learning professionals who work in organizations that use a balanced scorecard–style planning process have an advantage in that agreeing on meaningful measures is a fundamental part of the process, as is the alignment of strategies, results, objectives, and initiatives. Those who don't use balanced scorecards can still learn from those who do, including how to avoid some common problems with scorecards.

One essential requirement for learning professionals who want their discipline to be considered as a strategic business driver is that they be able to link organizational strategies to learning programs and outcomes. Being able to establish this link is vital when presenting learning options because otherwise you're asking decision makers to trust your judgment rather than presenting logical, business-minded arguments for your solution. The fewer connections you can establish between strategies and past results, the less likely it is that decision makers are going to believe that any such connection is ever going to exist.

To address this problem in a systematic way, it's necessary to have mechanisms in place that link organizational objectives, learning, and results during the planning process and to provide benchmarks and metrics for evaluating progress and performance over time. Such processes, once in place, make it considerably easier to explain the *why* of a learning initiative, as well as *who* it will affect and *what* its likely impact will be.

Beware of the ROI Trap

In their exhaustive efforts to develop a bullet-proof justification for investing in learning, many practitioners focus solely on trying to demonstrate a direct ROI. It's a noble goal, one that's often thought of as the key to gaining respect and credibility in any organization. We think there is a link that is just as important to establish, however, and that's the meaningful link between an organization's strategies and its learning programs and initiatives. If such a link exists, then your program will garner a return on the organization's investment—or else you're doing something wrong.

The reason such linkages are important is that when presenting learning, it's often more persuasive to be able to demonstrate training's *strategic impact* on the organization as a whole than it is to be able to create impressive ROI numbers. ROI is one piece of the impact puzzle, but it is by no means the entire picture. In fact, those who obsess about ROI risk falling into several hidden traps.

If ROI measurements aren't done very well or are superficial, they can distort the picture of what's really happening in the organization, affecting your credibility as a learning professional. Also, in many organizations, ROI is calculated as a defensive measure against the impulse to cut the training budget when times get tough. The numbers are used primarily to combat skepticism about the value of training initiatives, not to reinforce the idea that training is vital to an organization's overall success.

Reducing learning initiatives to a specific number can backfire in other ways as well. For one thing, it can lead top executives to the conclusion that training's benefits *can* be reduced only to a number, and that's all they need to know about it—a potentially disastrous perception if the investment numbers aren't favorable. Second, many upper executives, especially CEOs, mistrust learning ROI estimates as a matter of principle, because they are fully aware of the difficulties involved in obtaining such numbers.

We're not suggesting that you abandon all efforts to calculate ROI or that ROI numbers aren't valuable because they can be, especially if they are calculated responsibly and show evidence of progress and success. What we are suggesting is that *emphasizing* ROI is not necessarily the only or the most effective way to communicate learning's strategic value to the enterprise. A much more promising place to start is with communicating, well before ROI enters the picture, training's strategic relevance to the execution of an organization's mission and its systemic benefits throughout the organization.

A Partial Answer: The Balanced Scorecard

Most of the methods currently being adopted to link organizational strategy and learning results are based on the balanced scorecard method of organizational alignment introduced in Robert Kaplan's and David Norton's (1992) seminal article. In fact, the term "strategy-focused organization" is what Kaplan and Norton use to describe organizations that put strategic planning at the center of their management activities using multilevel, cross-functional planning teams who tap into knowledge and expertise at all levels of the organization.

Variations on the scorecard theme now have been developed for almost every imaginable role in organizational management. For example, Brian Becker, Mark Huselid, and Dave Ulrich (2001) created an HR scorecard, and ASTD released the workplace learning and performance (WLP) scorecard in 2007. (For more on ASTD's WLP scorecard, see next page.) In addition, there are versions of scorecards related to marketing, sales, training, accounting, and so on. Furthermore, organizations that adopt scorecard methodologies tailor them to their own purposes. For example, the University of Alabama school of optometry uses six different scorecards, depending upon which aspect of the discipline people are involved with.

In any case, a scorecard method of strategic planning opens up several leverage points for learning professionals that don't exist (at least not formally) in more traditional planning processes. It's at these leverage points where the proactive learning professional has the best opportunity to influence the way learning is funded, tracked, measured, and implemented. The sort of organizational reshuffling necessary to make such procedures possible doesn't happen instantaneously. In fact, companies who have taken this approach report that the effort can take three to five years to fully implement.

A Great Position to Be In

Once in place, the tasks of aligning an organization's strategies and objectives with its learning initiatives and measuring outcomes, financial or otherwise, all get integrated into the planning process. Scorecards don't solve every problem, but they are a useful tool for connecting the dots between strategies and results, which are connections that today's decision makers want to see.

For example, at Johnson Controls, director of learning and development Janice Simmons followed a course similar to David Vance's and is now reaping the rewards of that effort. It took her five years to transform the HR, training, and communication structure of her

ASTD's WLP Scorecard

In early 2007, ASTD launched a comprehensive and powerful online benchmarking and decision support tool for workplace learning and performance. The WLP scorecard provides instant comparisons on a broad range of learning and nonlearning variables, and diagnoses strengths and weaknesses of each organization. The WLP scorecard generates scorecard reports that cover financial, operations, customer, and innovation indicators, as well as index reports that provide diagnostics on the alignment, efficiency, effectiveness, and sustainability of the learning function.

The WLP scorecard is an online real-time benchmarking and decision support tool that allows organizations to

- monitor and benchmark a broad range of learning function financial, operations, customer, and innovation indicators
- customize reports with subsets of organizations and indicators
- compare the alignment, efficiency, effectiveness, and sustainability of an enterprise learning function, as well as the overall quality of the learning function, with hundreds of other organizations
- diagnose strengths and weaknesses in variables that affect alignment, efficiency, effectiveness, and sustainability
- perform sensitivity analysis to see potential effects of adjustments to multiple variables on alignment, efficiency, effectiveness, and sustainability
- make decisions about all aspects of learning, including investments, staffing, processes, and the type and amount of formal and work-based learning opportunities to provide.

organization into a fully functioning business consultancy network. She encountered some resistance at first from people who didn't want to talk to business leaders, or who preferred doing things their own way, but she eventually prevailed.

"For us, the hardest part was helping the existing learning and development team operate differently," says Simmons. "We spent a lot of time and energy... to change our behavior. From the moment

Caterpillar University

David Vance did not start out being able to assert confidently that Caterpillar University delivers $100 million in value to Caterpillar's bottom line and that the rate of ROI is roughly 200 percent. It took at least three years and involved a number of initiatives on his part that went well beyond the strict call of duty. Not only did he apply traditional evaluation methods for learning solutions, he diligently worked to quantify intangibles such as leadership ability and management skills by insisting that people estimate the value they received from a course or track and recording their answers over time. It involved developing a disciplined process for establishing goals and metrics, one that now involves developing an annual enterprise learning plan more than 100 pages long. But, mostly it involved an iron will on Vance's part to gather the necessary data to prove the University's contribution to the company, as well as plenty of confidence that the results would eventually speak for themselves.

"You can't do it overnight. It takes time," says Vance. His advice to those who want to build their credibility through measurable data is to take it slow, be methodical, be patient, and be humble.

He advises starting out with traditional training evaluation methods, and then "picking some metrics, doing some projections and estimates, and keeping track of them. See how the trends develop over a year or two or three, and don't pressure yourself to go too fast. Once you've gathered the data, be humble about the findings, even if your results are spectacular. Don't just share the good results either. If you want to build your credibility, share the good and the bad. Be honest about what is working and what isn't."

I arrived, it took three or four months before I understood the situation here. It took two or three years to change how we ran things, and a year and a half just to get some programs in place. After that, it took another year for people in the rest of the organization to get used to doing things differently." Now that everyone understands what they're doing and how they're doing it, she says, "we now get more requests than we can possibly handle. The organization wants so much from us that we can't possibly fulfill them. It's a great position to be in."

Simmons acknowledges that she had two enormous advantages in her favor: unqualified support from the top and an open checkbook. "My orders were to figure out how to get maximum value out of the company's learning and development efforts. I had no other restrictions," she says. For those who are not so fortunate, she advises starting small and taking it slow.

"In the beginning, pick one or two key programs—ones that have a strategic operations component—and work hard to make them successful," says Simmons. "Not everything has to be strategic, some of it can be tactical, but if it succeeds, your success will grow along with it. . . . A lot of projects come out of strategic work that is tactical or transitional. That doesn't make them any less important, though. It all needs to be done, and people should do it all to the best of their ability."

How Can Scorecards Help When Presenting Learning?

Besides being helpful in aligning strategy and initiatives, the great benefit of the scorecard method for learning professionals is that it introduces other types of measurement than strictly financial ones. It also reinforces a planning process that takes steps for measurement and targeting into account. Rather than jumping directly from a vision and mission to projects and initiatives, scorecard planning starts with the vision and desired results, then moves to strategies, measures of strategic performance that are based on outcomes and results, and then finally to the initiatives themselves.

An organization that uses a scorecard method for strategic planning must take measurements and targets into account as a fundamental part of the process, which gives learning professionals the opportunity to discuss measurements and the means for acquiring them before the actual initiatives have even been decided upon. Done correctly, this approach can alleviate at least three of the learning professional's most vexing problems:

- the expectation that high-level performance and results data can somehow be squeezed out of low-level measurement methods

- the criticism that learning has little tangible value or that its contribution to the organization cannot be reliably measured

- the idea that learning is not an integral part of the strategic operations of the organization.

Figure 8-1 is an example of a balanced-scorecard-type planning chart for a regional airline. The strategic vision of the airline is to keep building on its unique position as "the only short-haul, low-fare, high-frequency, point-to-point carrier in America." The theme of this score-card is "operating efficiency," and the card is read from left to right. Notice that the strategic objective—greater operating efficiency—is in the left-hand column, whereas the actual initiatives are in the right-hand column. Between them are objectives, measures, and targets.

In this example, learning is on the bottom row, but as you can see by the arrows, the entire value chain depends upon the need to "align ground crews," which will help "improve turnaround times," which will lead to more on-time flights, the ability to serve more customers, and ultimately increased revenue and profits. Of course, learning is only part of the process, and there are other initiatives and targets that other people need to worry about, but this balanced scorecard shows that learning is clearly an integral and organic part of the airline's operations, one that feeds into the airline's internal operations, customer relations, and financial picture.

In the next column to the right, "objectives," the learning objective is "ground crew alignment." If you were part of the planning process, the question you would have asked at this point in the process would be, "What will ground crew alignment look like?" The answer to that question would have been: "100 percent of the ground crew would be stockholders in the company (giving them a greater sense of ownership),

Figure 8-1. Example of a balanced scorecard for a regional airline.

Mission: Dedication to the highest quality of Customer Service delivered with a sense of warmth, friendliness, individual pride, and company spirit.

Vision: Continue building on our unique position—the only short-haul, low-fare, high-frequency, point-to-point carrier in America.

Theme: Operating Efficiency	Objectives	Measures	Targets	Initiatives
Financial	• Profitability • Fewer planes • Increased revenue	• Market value • Seat revenue • Plane lease cost	• 24% per year • 20% per year • 5% per year	• Optimize routes • Standardize planes
Customer	• Flight is on time • Lowest prices • More customers	• FAA on time arrival rating • Customer ranking • Number of customers	• First in industry • 96% Satisfaction • % Change	• Quality management • Customer loyalty program
Internal	• Fast ground turnaround	• On ground time • On-time departure	• < 25 minutes • 93%	• Cycle time optimization program
Learning	• Ground crew alignment	• % Ground crew stockholders • % Ground crew trained	• year 1: 70% • year 4: 90% • year 6: 100%	• Stock ownership plan • Ground crew training

Source: Reprinted with permission from the Balanced Scorecard Institute, 2006.

and 100 percent of the ground crew would be fully trained." The "measures" for accomplishing those goals would be the percentage of ground crew workers who were actually stockholders and the percentage of ground crew workers who were fully trained.

If upper management went into this planning process believing that all of the objectives could be accomplished in a year, that's where negotiations over what should be measured, how, and for how long would come into play. As the learning professional in charge of negotiations, you would have pointed out that although it is reasonable to train ground crew members as they come on board with the company, the stockholder initiative would be more complicated. You would have done your homework to find out how similar programs have been implemented in other companies, and you would have had that data with you to demonstrate that a reasonable expectation in the first year would be 70 percent adoption, but that, judging from the experience of others who have tried it, nabbing that other 30 percent would take considerably more effort and time. Realistically, you think you could get 90 percent after four years, and 100 percent after six years, when vested employees really start to see the full benefits of the program.

So, before you have even discussed what sort of stock ownership plan to implement or how to educate employees about it, you've already had a discussion about realistic measurements and estimated timeframes. Those measurements and timeframes might change if you found ways to accelerate adoption of the program—through some sort of vacation incentive, say (you're an airline, after all)—but, the point is that going through a planning process like this opens up the opportunity for dialog about measurements and targets much earlier in the decision cycle, making it much less likely for you to get trapped trying to reach an impossible goal with inadequate resources. And, by working in the order of strategy, objectives, measures, and *then* initiatives, rather than vice versa, the link between the initiative and the strategy is easy to see, and the line ultimately linking the initiative to its impact on profitability can be easily traced as well.

This scorecard is simplified for purposes of illustration. As anyone who has ever done it can tell you, the process of creating such a scorecard in a large organization with different departments and conflicting agendas is no picnic. Nevertheless, going through the process of thinking about how objectives and initiatives in one part of the organization affect those in other parts of the organization, and how they all integrate into the whole is a vital step toward breaking down silos and getting executives and managers to think systemically and holistically. It also introduces into the planning process measurable checks and balances to ensure that organizations and departments are being run on sound business principles and that not all the decisions are being made on the basis of past performance measures, so-called lagging indicators. Instead, objectives, measures, and targets are forward focused, providing a kind of roadmap to the future. The scorecard method opens up opportunities for learning professionals to dialog with managers in other parts of the organization to assess their needs, understand more deeply how learning influences employees, discover skill and performance gaps that need to be addressed, and ultimately align whatever learning is deemed appropriate with the strategies, goals, and activities of the rest of the organization.

What If You Can't Use a Scorecard?

If your organization does not use a balanced-scorecard-type system and isn't likely to implement one anytime soon, you can take comfort from the fact that there are other ways to think about organizational decision making.

One way to gain the advantage of a scorecard without actually having one is to keep asking questions about measures and targets early in the process. Insist that to be effective, you need to know what sort of measurements are necessary, how these measurements will be done, and what the targets or benchmarks are *before* you can responsibly design or implement a program. Strive to make the measurement piece inseparable from the program itself; it's in your best interest to do so,

W. Edwards Deming: Grandfather of the Scorecard

Although scorecard systems are thought of as a relatively recent management phenomenon, the ideas behind the balanced scorecard have been
percolating in academic and management circles since at least the 1950s,
when W. Edwards Deming, after World War II, began working with
Japanese management teams to apply various statistical methodologies
to industrial production and management. Deming's methods and ideas
about measurement-based management, innovation, process improvement, quality control, and employee empowerment are widely credited
with helping spark the innovation revolution that transformed Japan into a
major manufacturing powerhouse during the 1970s and 1980s.

Deming is the one who first encouraged executives to think of
organizations as complex systems rather than bits and pieces of machin-
ery that work together, and it was Deming who first adopted the idea that
quality, even on the floor of an automobile factory, is largely a reflection
of management skills, not the skills of laborers on the shop floor. Deming
also insisted that human beings could not be treated like machines, that
to do so was counterproductive, and that tapping into the knowledge and
expertise of employees throughout an organization was the way to spark
innovation and improve quality.

Interestingly, about the same time that Kaplan and Norton started
publishing about balanced scorecards, Deming was creating the W.
Edwards Deming Institute in Washington, D.C., to help advance a 14-point
system of management ideas he developed in the 1980s, which he called
the Deming System of Profound Knowledge.

Deming was famous for saying, "The worker is not the problem.
The problem is at the top! Management!... It is management's job to
direct the efforts of all components toward the aim of the system. The
first step is clarification: Everyone in the organization must understand
the aim of the system, and how to direct his efforts toward it" (CC-M
Productions, 2006). By that, he meant that whatever management does
ripples through the rest of an organization; therefore, the way to prevent
off-target or out-of-sync ripples is to align the communication from the

top with everything below it and to cascade consistent messages from level to level, and from worker to worker. Presentation Mastery is based on similar ideas about the benefits of focused messaging and increased productivity through a clear understanding of strategy and consistent reinforcement of the right messages, delivered in the proper way, to the right people, at the right time.

"An aim without a method is useless. A method without an aim is dangerous," Deming once wrote, and a truer statement about the importance of linking strategies with actions has yet to be written.

and insisting on it will signal to upper management that you are serious about aligning learning and performance with the organization's strategic objectives and about tracking the results and impact of learning on the enterprise.

This is important because one of the most frustrating paradoxes that learning professionals face is a demand from the top that the results of learning be tracked and measured, combined with an unwillingness by those making the demands to invest in the resources necessary to perform those metrics and skepticism about the numbers when they do come. To get reliable bottom-line evaluations of learning requires organizational resources in terms of personnel and funds. Unless management provides such backing, learning professionals are left in an uncomfortable position, trying to draw conclusions from insufficient data while being criticized for a lack of certainty about learning's impact on the organization.

Those who want to break free of this paradoxical trap must often devise their own game plan for getting the metrics they need with the limited resources they have. If the effort does not receive the blessing of upper management, it might have to be done covertly, in a gradual but persistent effort that takes patience and dedication to execute. Even in organizations that support and fund sophisticated levels of measurement, an effort must still be made to gradually educate upper executives on the meaning and value of the data derived from the effort because all too often an overabundance of data leads frugal executives to conclude that there is waste and inefficiency in all those piles of paper.

To some extent, almost all learning professionals are engaged in an ongoing effort to legitimize and enhance the worth of their efforts. Inside an organization, the urgency of this project might range from a desperate bid for survival to a concerted, organized effort to transform the department into the sort of proactive, business partner model toward which most forward-thinking organizations are gravitating. From the outside, obtaining quantifiable information about the effectiveness of one's efforts on behalf of an organization can be challenging, especially getting data or testimonials about one's effectiveness over the long haul.

Remember, Communication Is the Goal

Whatever the circumstances are, remember that the ultimate goal of developing any type of measurement system or set of metrics is communication. Senior executives want communication from managers about what is working and what isn't. Metrics are simply one way of supplying that information, a sort of numerical shorthand that tells executive decision makers what they want to know.

Looked at in this way, the demand from the top for meaningful metrics doesn't seem quite so punitive. Executives don't like making decisions on blind faith, so it's in the learning function's best interests to provide any quantifiable evidence of value to the enterprise and help devise acceptable tools for obtaining that information.

In doing so, however, learning professionals also need to develop a deep understanding that the value they contribute *can* and should be quantified. Far too many people in the learning profession are afraid that if they are held accountable to the bottom line, they will come up short, and management will have a handy excuse to get rid of them. The truth is that a well-managed, well-run learning department—as well as a top-notch coach or consultant—is going to return tremendous value to any organization. Most measurements of that activity are going to land squarely in the black.

Those who *should* be afraid of what the numbers might say are those who aren't running disciplined learning departments, who don't pay attention to business realities, and whose programs aren't developed or deployed in ways that effectively support the organization and its goals. In such instances, decision makers are entirely justified in their calls for restructuring and change. Departments that don't deliver value to the bottom line *should* be reorganized. Coaches and consultants who do not bring a significant value with them when they walk through the door *shouldn't* be hired. The numbers should communicate a positive story, and that story should be the truth: that the organization's learning and development efforts are effective, cost-efficient, and impactful. If they're not, work needs to be done to make them so. Then you will be in a perfect position to deliver the good news.

Is There a Downside to the Scorecard Approach?

Balanced scorecards are not the cure for everything and can even lead to problems of their own. For example, at the J.B. Hunt trucking company, one of the complaints of truck drivers was that their line supervisors didn't spend enough time with them and always seemed rushed to get to the next person. However, when the line supervisors were asked about the issue of time spent with drivers, they reported that their scorecards only allowed them to spend a short amount of time with each driver; otherwise, they would get hopelessly behind. This is a classic case of conflicting measurements, and it is not uncommon to have similar problems in any organization. Determining the right measures that deliver the desired results for the organization is one of the most important responsibilities of leadership.

Very Important Points

- Learning professionals need to walk their own talk in terms of setting clear goals and measuring outcomes.
- Flexibility and responsiveness are the keys to success in 21st-century learning. Don't cling to old habits and familiar programs. Be open to new solutions and ways of doing things.

■ Balanced scorecard planning processes help learning professionals by putting the issue of measurement, targets, and benchmarks front and center so they can be discussed and agreed upon before other programming commitments are made.

■ Scorecards broaden the palette of meaningful measurements available, reducing the reliance on purely financial data to prove learning's value.

■ When presenting learning, use the scorecard process to influence the way learning programs are measured and implemented.

■ Transforming a traditional learning function into one that operates according to stricter business disciplines and as a proactive business partner takes time, but it is well worth the effort. Experts advise taking it slowly and establishing success one program at a time.

■ Those who don't used scorecards can adapt some of the core ideas by forcing the discussion of metrics, targets, and benchmarks earlier in the decision-making process.

Using a balanced scorecard approach gives you a logical framework for aligning learning initiatives with your organization's strategic goals and for setting up measures and targets that can serve as a basis for evaluating the success of your initiatives. Once that foundation is firmly in place, your job becomes one of persuading decision makers that learning is indeed a strategic driver of value and that learning and development are operating in concert with your organization's goals and objectives. The next chapter focuses on just that: the power of persuasion.

9

Persuasion for Learning Professionals

To the Point

Providing statistics, great content, and a solid business case aren't all learning professionals need to progress in the 21st-century organization. It also helps to have some skills of persuasion. Robert Cialdini,* a professor of social science at Arizona State University, is an eminent authority on the social science of persuasion. He has discovered that the psychology of persuasion can be broken down into six basic principles. You've already read about one of them—reciprocity—in chapter 5. In this chapter, we'll explain the other five and discuss how learning professionals can apply these principles of persuasion in practical situations.

*Adapted with permission from Robert Cialdini, the author of *Influence: Science and Practice* (2000, Allyn & Bacon).

One of the main reasons why learning professionals covet a seat at the table is to influence the outcome of important decisions that affect the organization's overall ability to achieve its objectives by highlighting ways that the learning function can work strategically to achieve those aims. Before that can happen, however, decision makers must be persuaded that learning is indeed a strategic driver of value and that learning and development are operating in concert with, and in support of, the organization's goals and objectives. This outcome won't happen by itself; it will only happen through great work, organizational alignment, and powerful persuasion.

We've already discussed work and alignment issues; now it's time to talk about persuasion. Many people think of the powers of persuasion as something that only salespeople need to use, but nothing could be further from the truth. In fact, most presentation situations involve some element of persuasion because most of the time you, as the presenter, are trying to get people to see things from your point of view. Learning professionals are often in persuasion mode, perhaps trying to convince upper management that undertaking a program or initiative is a worthwhile investment or, for example, to sell new recruits on the importance of some safety measure. Outside consultants must also persuade organizations that their services are valuable, or else they'll have no one with whom to consult.

Why Persuasion Isn't the Same as Selling

The whole idea of persuasion makes many people uncomfortable, however. "I could never be in sales" is a typical thing to hear. Persuasion is often associated with the sometimes manipulative, aggressive, and annoying tactics of some types of salesmanship. Persuasion is a much more subtle and sophisticated art than mere salesmanship, though. Salespeople want people to say yes to whatever they're selling; they don't focus on changing their customers' attitudes, behaviors, preferences, biases or habits, except as it relates to their product or service. Persuasion has more to do with winning another person's confidence and trust. It involves a much broader range of human behaviors, as well as a much more sophisticated awareness of psychological cues and motivators. Leaders use it to motivate those whom they are leading. Managers use it to get the best out of their people. In the marketplace of ideas, a persuasive presentation is as important as the idea itself, and the two often go hand in hand.

In the largest sense, persuasion is about wielding influence and power effectively. In a company or any other type of organization, it involves building strong personal relationships and developing networks of influence that can bolster a case for a proposal, advance new ideas, or sway decision makers. Persuasion is the force that moves markets and makes things happen one way or another. Those who are experts at persuasion know how to make sure that the balance leans in their favor most of the time. They are able to do this because they don't look at negotiations in quite the same way as other people, and they don't respond to conflict or resistance in quite the same ways either. For instance, many professionals giving a presentation might be flustered by a CEO who asks blunt questions about their programs, credentials, or value to the company. Someone schooled in the art of persuasion simply looks at such questions—even if they come in the form of overt resistance—as requests for more information, no more and no less. Emotion doesn't enter into it; objections and resistance are just indicators that the other person needs more information to come to the right conclusion.

We all want to be the sort of person who knows exactly what to say in every situation, particularly situations in which one has an urgent stake in the outcome. If you want to be one of those people, it helps to understand some of the underlying psychological principles of persuasion and how one might apply them in professional situations. Indeed, Presentation Masters use them all the time in spontaneous, unconscious ways that over time have become a natural part of their personality. Knowledge of the psychology of persuasion is not a magic solution to every problem by any means, but it can help guide your thinking and behavior in situations where persuasion is involved. Furthermore, such knowledge can help you to understand better why people do things or react in one way rather than another, all of which can help you become a better, more persuasive Presentation Master.

In chapter 5, we introduced one of Cialdini's principles of persuasion, the principle of reciprocity, the idea that people feel compelled to repay gifts or favors they receive from others. There are, however, five other fundamental principles of persuasion of which every learning professional should be aware (Cialdini, 2000). The six principles are

1. **C**onsistency

2. **L**iking

3. **A**uthority

4. **S**ocial proof

5. **S**carcity

6. **R**eciprocity.

It's easy to remember the principles using the acronym CLASS R but how you remember them is not as important as understanding how you can apply them in real-life situations.

The Principle of Consistency

The principle of consistency states that people have a strong desire to remain consistent with their previous opinions, assertions, and actions. People don't want to be hypocrites, they don't like to change their mind, and they don't like to reverse themselves on positions on which they have already taken a public stand. Research also shows that people are much more likely to adhere to a position or principle if they have written it down, and they are most likely to remain loyal to themselves if they have not only written something down, but also have shown it to others.

Practical Application

Suppose you are negotiating the details of a learning initiative, but those you are negotiating with have a record of backsliding or not following through on previous promises. To secure a commitment that is more likely to stick, both parties should agree to terms in writing, each party should be witness to the agreement, and at least one other party should witness it as well. In the midst of negotiations, the principle of consistency also makes it a bad idea to state one's bottom line too early. Again, people don't like to retreat from previously stated positions and often corner themselves into taking a stand, even if it's a bad idea to do so. If you are aware of a senior executive's previous position or opinion on a particular type of initiative or issue, you can use his or her previous position as leverage for support for the one you're proposing. Their support isn't guaranteed, but the principle of consistency makes it more likely that they will side with you if your proposal is aligned with their previously stated position.

The Principle of Liking

The principle of liking states that people are more easily influenced by people they like and whom they perceive are like them. This may sound obvious, but it's a truth many people fail to appreciate. How powerful is it? In one case, researchers mailed a set of surveys to random individuals. The surveys were accompanied by a cover letter. Half the surveys were signed by an actual researcher, but the other half were "signed" by a "researcher" with a name purposely similar to the recipient's. Other than the signatures, the surveys were identical, but people filled out the surveys signed by the researcher with a similar name twice as often. This is one reason why salespeople are coached to say people's names while talking to them. There are other useful applications as well.

Practical Application

When Presentation Masters talk to people about their work and lives, they instinctively look for some kind of personal connection to help solidify the relationship. When they do this, they are using the principle of liking to build rapport and, incidentally, gain an advantage in the persuasion game. It's also why, if you want to start building a personal relationship with your CEO or anyone else, you should find out what he or she likes in the way of food, books, music, movies, recreation, travel, business philosophy, or whatever, and let it be known when you share genuine interests. The principle of liking can also be used to build consensus. Saying something such as, "Do you agree with Sheryl that this is a really great program?" is more persuasive than just saying, "Do you think this is a great program?" because if the person you're talking to likes Sheryl, disagreeing about the program would also mean disagreeing with Sheryl.

The Principle of Authority

The principle of authority is simple: People are more likely to be influenced by people they perceive to be legitimate authorities. The principle of authority is why police officers wear uniforms and doctors hang their diplomas on the wall; these are outward symbols of individual authority, and the perceived legitimacy of a person's power is the key. To gain that legitimacy, people must typically have the type of experience, skill, or education required for the position, and their authority must be acknowledged publicly in some way. This competence establishes their credibility and inspires trust, which is an essential element of persuasion.

Practical Application

The great mistake most people make with regard to the principle of authority is assuming that their own authority is somehow self-evident. It often isn't, in which case it must be established. Presentation Masters establish their authority in several ways. With larger audiences, the best way to confer instant credibility on a speaker is to have someone who already has credibility with the audience introduce him or her. In one-on-one or small group situations, people must usually do the heavy lifting themselves, either by alluding to previous experience in certain areas or by referring to information they could only know if they actually were an expert. When Masters seek to frame discussions with a certain context, one of the contexts that must be established is the one related to authority. That's why it's important to have data, facts, research, comparisons with the competition, and other information at your fingertips; that information reinforces your credibility as an expert, putting you in a position to exert your influence.

The Principle of Social Proof

When deciding how to act in a given situation, one of the ways people decide what to do is to look around them and see what others in the same situation are doing or have done. The old television show "Candid Camera" used to exploit this tendency by instructing a group of people to do something odd—such as hop on one foot—and then send an unsuspecting person into the group to see how long it was before he or she began hopping on one foot. This "when in Rome" impulse is strongest in situations where there is a great deal of uncertainty. Executives face uncertainty all of the time, of course, which means that social proof can often be used to persuade them.

Practical Application

One of the things executives do to decide which action to take next is to see what others—executives of other companies, for instance, particularly the competition—are doing. Consequently, one of the most persuasive things a Presentation Master can do is scout the competition first and, if their performance is better in some key area, report what they are doing, how they are doing it, and the best way to catch up. This is a mandatory step when discussing initiatives that are new, odd, or out of the ordinary. Nobody wants to be a guinea pig for failure; but, similarly, no one wants to be left in the dust. That's why sharing best practices is so powerful; everyone wants to be the best, so everyone imitates those who are deemed to be the best.

Learning professionals should also keep social proof in mind as an influential force in shaping corporate culture. By spotlighting successful people and modeling the most productive practices in a profession, trainers can use the principle of social proof to encourage new or reluctant employees to imitate that successful behavior. Social proof is also one of the reasons that Presentation Masters spend so much time building consensus for their ideas and programs. It's because they know that the more people they have in their corner, the more social proof they can leverage.

The Principle of Scarcity

In 1985, when Coca-Cola announced that it was retiring its 99-year-old recipe in favor of a sweeter soft-drink blend called New Coke, consumer demand for the original Coca-Cola skyrocketed. The company claims not to have planned it this way, but the principle of scarcity still worked in its favor. Simply put, the principle of scarcity means that the less accessible a thing is, the more desirable and often the more valuable the thing becomes. The old adage, "If you want to be popular, make yourself scarce," has more than a little truth in it. Products and people aren't the only places where this principle applies, however; it can also be a factor when deciding on ideas, strategies, and learning initiatives.

Practical Application

One of the ways in which successful salespeople ply their trade is by describing the unique characteristics or advantages of their product or service or by convincing people that a certain item is selling fast and soon will be gone. One reason that the word "sale" is so powerful is that in addition to offering a price break on merchandise, it also implies that availability of the items on sale is temporary. ("Buy now: quantities are limited!") When negotiating a learning plan or discussing a program, you can leverage the idea of scarcity by describing the otherwise unattainable benefits of the plan or program, or emphasizing the unique competitive advantages it will give the organization. Furthermore, research on scarcity also suggests that it's more persuasive to emphasize what will be lost if some action isn't taken. This can be particularly powerful when talking about the lost intangibles of ineffective or inadequate training, such as lost morale, lost opportunities, lost leadership, and so forth.

Use Persuasion Principles Responsibly

If you stop to examine them, you can see the principles of persuasion at work (or not) in almost any presentation situation. However, in his seminars, Cialdini is always careful to remind people that there are honest, principled ways to use the psychology of persuasion, as well as dishonest, unprincipled ways. It is important to draw a distinction between acceptable uses of influence and objectionable, deceptive uses. For example, using the principles to consciously trick, manipulate, or trap people into agreeing with you is ethically wrong and can backfire in any number of ways. Dealing with people dishonestly or pressuring them into doing things they don't really want to do damages the foundation of trust necessary to work effectively with people, reflects badly on professionals who do it, and, ultimately, is counterproductive.

If used properly, however, these same principles can be used constructively to influence decisions and lead to better choices. If people's similarities are genuine, their authority legitimate, the social proof real, and the commitments or agreements made on either side are entered into willingly and in good faith, the resulting choices and decisions can be win-win solutions for everyone.

Another reason Presentation Masters do not misuse the principles of persuasion is because they know that people who feel coerced or manipulated usually harbor anger and resentment toward the person who twisted their arm. Such feelings work against someone who is trying to seed goodwill and initiate a cycle of positive momentum. The Masters also know that pretending to be someone you're not, backing ideas or programs you don't really believe in, or otherwise acting dishonestly to throw your weight around, is ultimately self-defeating. It's the dark side of the power of influence. Always avoid polluting your communication with ill-advised attempts to abuse the psychology of persuasion for your own personal gain.

In the real world, of course, the principles of persuasion do not come so neatly packaged. They overlap and conflict with each other in various ways, many of them unpredictable, and some of them just plain confusing. For example, if you go out to coffee with someone to discuss a project, you may be using the principle of liking to build rapport, the principles of social proof and consistency to solidify consensus and agreement, the principle of scarcity to emphasize the importance of a program, and the principle of reciprocity when you pick up the tab. All these factors work together to determine degrees of influence, but they are not 100-percent accurate predictors of behavior. Rather, they are ways of breaking down complex human behavior into a manageable body of theory. In practice, Presentation Masters internalize these principles until they are second nature, and use them in situations where persuasion and negotiation are paramount. Masters do not think of these ideas as separate principles; they are just part of the psychological portfolio of forces that exist when more than one person in a room is responsible for making a decision.

Learning professionals who want to be more persuasive in their dealings with colleagues, clients, superiors, or anyone else can start by simply observing the behavior of people in everyday situations. Notice what sorts of behavior people respond positively to and pay particular attention to things that upset or annoy them. As with the DiSC system of personality profiles, it takes some practice to see human behavior through the lens of persuasion, but once you start noticing real-world instances of these principles in action, you will begin to appreciate their universal nature. If you have teenagers, for instance, the principle of social proof is on display every day in the way they dress, the music they listen to, and the friends with whom they choose to hang out. If you want to see the principle of scarcity in action, simply take away a child's toy; it will suddenly become the most important thing in the world to that child. Things aren't too terribly different in the boardroom, where executives spend a great deal of their time looking over their collective shoulders to see what the other guys—the competition—are doing and wondering if they should be doing it too.

The point is to learn what you can from the principles of persuasion, have fun with them, and start slowly incorporating them into your thinking. Over time, you will begin to appreciate the many ways in which they explain the behavior of those around you. The more you understand what motivates people with whom you are communicating, the better you will be at connecting with them in a way that yields more positive outcomes and more desirable results.

Very Important Points

- To be an influencing factor in any organization, especially at the "table" where decisions are made, you need to develop strong powers of persuasion.

- Don't mistake the art of persuasion with selling. The two are different things.

- If you want to be more persuasive in overcoming resistance, start viewing questions and expressions of concern as probes for more information, nothing more. Keep the emotion contained.

- Robert Cialdini's six principles of persuasion can be remembered using the acronym CLASS R: Consistency, Liking, Authority, Social proof, Scarcity, and Reciprocity.

- To learn how the principles of persuasion operate in everyday life, start observing those around you through the lens of persuasion.

- Remember to apply the principles of persuasion responsibly, in good faith, and with sincere intentions. Using them for purposes of manipulation, coercion, or deception will inevitably backfire.

We've described here the psychological basis for using persuasion to your advantage as you present your learning and development proposals to your organization's decision makers. The next chapter goes into more detail about how you can use metaphors, analogies, and storytelling to paint a picture of what success will look like and construct a case for learning that doesn't depend entirely on numbers using some special techniques.

10

Making Intangibles Tangible

To the Point

If you don't have data or other tangible evidence to support your ideas, it helps to be adept at illustrating the benefits of learning in other ways. Through metaphors, analogies, and storytelling, it's possible to paint a picture of what success will look like and make a persuasive case for learning that doesn't depend entirely on numbers. We also present several ways to make the intangible benefits of learning come to life. Learning professionals who want to advance their careers should learn how to use these techniques to construct more persuasive, compelling arguments.

Strong learning programs can yield tremendous benefits that sometimes are not clearly recognized at the top. Companies that invest in learning tend to have higher morale because employees feel confident in their ability to do the job for which they have been hired, and it's easier to feel good about an organization that thinks enough of its employees to invest in their professional development. Effective learning programs can also go a long way toward cementing the company's culture and instilling a strong sense of loyalty among the staff. The strongest cultures, which tend to grow out of the strongest programs, are able to instill a kind of missionary zeal in associates, a sense of purpose so strong that it's infectious and energizing.

It's hard to measure energy, though. It's sometimes difficult to explain even the most basic benefits of a learning program in ways that will make people sit up and take notice. Other times, little is available in the way of supporting data, making it difficult to assess the strength of a program or build a strong business case. Other times, the benefits of a program don't accrue for months or even years.

In such cases, it can be helpful to use other techniques for bringing ideas to life, techniques that engage the listener's imagination and, if done well, get them emotionally involved. Learning professionals can put these techniques to good use because many of the subjects they talk about often—the value of learning, the power of knowledge, the heights of human potential—are not easily captured in charts or bullet points.

Use Compelling Metaphors and Analogies

For example, rather than going over the details of a program to the nth degree and risk losing your audience in the process, it can be helpful to use metaphors and analogies to get your point across. Workplace learning professionals often are challenged to assess the results of programs that promise to develop strong leadership. Intuitively, everyone understands that strong leadership is desirable, but the process of creating leaders is an inexact science at best. If you were to compare leadership to what happens when you're baking bread, you could make this complicated process seem simple. For example, you might say, "If you put some flour, water, and salt together, you have 99 percent of the ingredients you need to make a loaf of bread. But, if you mix it together and put it in the oven, it will bake up into a hard, inedible brick. To make bread out of it, you have to add yeast and let it bubble for a while, knead it into shape, and then put it in the oven. This leadership program is like the yeast. We have 99 percent of the ingredients we need for success. Now all we need to do is put this program in to the mix, let it do its magic, and see the results."

The value of knowledge to an organization is another subject that frustrates learning professionals because tracking and evaluating what people learn and how they apply that new knowledge to their jobs and the associated results can be very difficult. Gardening and other nature metaphors are good ways to illustrate effects on the organizational ecosystem. An example: "We all know that knowledge is important and that what we do with it is the key to our survival. But why is that so? What is knowledge and how does it work? I look at it this way: Consider two different gardeners with identical plants, soil, and water. They can both create a nice-looking garden, but if you give one gardener fertilizer for her plants, in a month or two her garden will look significantly more robust. The plants will be larger, there will be more flowers, and all of her fruit and vegetables will be larger. Knowledge in an organization is like that fertilizer; it spreads invisibly but strengthens and grows everything it touches."

Personal anecdotes can also be powerful in a presentation. Metaphors and analogies can come from anywhere. All one has to do is think about the similarities between something in everyday life and the issues you face at the office, compare them in a meaningful way, and—presto!—you've just made that boring business matter more interesting. Metaphors and analogies only work if they crystallize the issue you're talking about in an interesting way, though. Keep them short and to the point, and don't allow yourself to digress too far from your main theme. Also, avoid extending metaphors too far; one or two connections is all most metaphors can credibly carry.

Presentation Masters make a habit of collecting stories, anecdotes, jokes, analogies, quotes, aphorisms, and other tidbits of information to illustrate various points or issues. Many professional speakers keep a notebook with them to record thoughts and ideas on the fly. Others keep stacks of 3-by-5 cards handy in case inspiration strikes, and many type notes into their personal digital assistant when they want to remember something. When collecting these ideas, the key is to write them down somewhere, anywhere, when they occur to you; otherwise they will be lost into the ether, and when you need them most, you won't be able to remember them.

Tell True Stories

True stories that illustrate a point can be just as powerful as a good metaphor. For example, you might single out something that happened as an indirect result of training: "As you know, six months ago we completed a companywide upgrade of our email system, which now includes an online calendar function. In addition to the overall training for every employee, each department volunteered two people for extra training to become champions of the system. The idea for these champions was to enable them to answer simple questions, so that the information technology people could focus on more complicated issues. It worked. In fact, it worked so well down in sales that Sue Schultz has figured out how to coordinate, schedule, and deploy her entire sales team using the system. At a glance, she can now see where everyone on her team is and knows their entire call schedule for the day. Last week, one of her people had a family emergency. She needed someone to cover a call fast. In two minutes, she was able to identify another associate three blocks away who could cover the call, and the result was a hefty new one-year contract. I think you'll agree that's the kind of speed, flexibility, and resourcefulness we want to encourage wherever we can."

Such stories don't just illustrate *what* happened, they also explain *how* and *why* it happened, none of which can be deduced from a number.

Insight into how business challenges are being addressed and resolved is of keen interest to executives. If you can link stories directly or indirectly to an important financial measure—revenue, profit, sales—or to an improvement in efficiency or productivity, so much the better.

Gather Testimonials

Another powerful way to reinforce an argument is to use testimonials. If you're a consultant or coach who has been working for a while, you probably already have a file drawer full of testimonials because they are important to establishing your credibility with new clients. You know the power of testimonials. Those working inside an organization can borrow a page from the consultant's playbook and gather their own testimonials.

You've already read that one great way to get executives to appreciate the intangibles of training is to get them involved in the training either as subject matter experts or as subjects of the training themselves. Participation is effective because it provides a visceral, firsthand experience that can't be obtained any other way. Some of the best-in-class programs are where executives are teaching: "Leaders as Teachers." In effect, while participating, executives create their own testimonials, and testimonials from upper executives are what you need if you expect to seed a learning culture that will take root and grow.

Lacking testimonials from the president or CEO, the next best thing is gathering testimonials from line managers or anyone else who is willing to talk about the benefits of personal learning experiences. Capturing good testimonials is surprisingly easy, and it's a wonder more people don't do it because testimonials can be extremely persuasive.

Most workplace learning professionals gather testimonials by filing away training evaluation forms (smile sheets) on which someone took the time to write a sentence or two. If you want to go the extra mile, you can email participants and ask for their input in writing. But, if you really want their testimonials to make a difference—if you want testimonials that will have a persuasive impact in a presentation—either videotape or audio-record them.

Leverage the Power of Video

The persuasive power of video, particularly in business situations, is highly underrated. *Presentations* magazine did a study in partnership with 3M to assess the persuasion power of multimedia (Simons, 2000). In one part of the study, people were given information about the services of three fictitious banks. The information about one bank was distributed through a brochure, another through static PowerPoint slides, and another through PowerPoint slides with a video testimonial from the bank president. When asked which bank had better services, nine out of 10 people said the bank with the video testimonial even though, in reality, the services offered by the banks were identical!

This is just one indication of video's power to persuade. In a business situation, video's power is magnified because it is largely unexpected. People go into most business presentations expecting to see a bunch of dull slides and hear a well-meaning presenter read the slides to the audience. Unfortunately, the brain short-circuits when slide after slide containing lists of bullet points is displayed on a screen and someone reads the slides aloud. No wonder people yawn as soon as the lights are dimmed for yet another slide presentation.

But, throw a few video clips up on the screen, showing employees talking about what they got out of a training program, and it's a different story. People perk up, pay attention, and they sense the importance and relevance of the information being presented. Voice recordings can have a similar impact, but video is best because it shows an actual human being talking, and training is ultimately about people, not numbers. One cannot measure the value of such a testimonial in dollars, but there is tremendous value in communicating the elusive human dimension of learning. Besides, what many CEOs want to see just as eagerly as encouraging numbers is evidence that *employees themselves* believe the training is valuable. Spreadsheets, meetings, and offices on a separate floor isolate upper executives from the working buzz of a company. What video can communicate is a feel for the pulse of the organization through some of its own people. It's a window to something CEOs rarely see, which is an employee speaking candidly to them about something in their company. Video is hard to squeeze in if time is limited, but any presentation more than 15 minutes long has room for a minute or two of footage.

Cheap, Easy, and Powerful

Video is ridiculously cheap and easy to shoot and edit, too. Many learning departments have a camcorder, and some companies will even make an audiovisual technician available. And clips don't have to be cleverly produced. In fact, it's often more effective if there is an amateurish quality to the video, because raw video feels more genuine. Videos that are too slickly produced can have the "feel" of advertising propaganda, and you don't want that. What you want is an honest, credible person testifying *in his or her own words* what he or she liked about the learning and got out of it. Fifteen or 20 seconds of footage is all you need to get a point across through any single person.

Such interviews don't have to be about a specific program, either. They can be gathered during preliminary interviews while doing your due diligence to identify skills gaps and other development needs. Keep files of them on your computer, arranged by topic, and they can be used in any number of presentation scenarios. You must ask for permission from the subjects in the video, of course, but most employees are more than happy to help out a colleague if it's for the good of the organization. Younger employees are particularly amenable because they grew up posting digital images and videos of themselves on the Internet. Ask around and you'll discover that people under 35 don't have the same reflexive shyness about appearing in video as those over 35. Of course, it could simply be that they *look better* than we older folks, but we're fairly certain there are other cultural factors at work here. There's a reason Google bought YouTube.com, and why millions of kids now communicate with each other on such websites as MySpace.com and Facebook.com. All of the technology has matured, so communicating personal messages visually is no longer the exception; it's becoming the rule.

If You Don't Have Data, Be Honest About It

The trouble with intangible benefits is that they are hard to count, measure, or track. Exactly how they affect the organization might be hard to say, but it's OK to admit it! Truthfully state that certain criteria are difficult, if not impossible, to measure. That way, you immediately relieve any pressure to provide numbers. Also, if it's appropriate, offer a brief explanation of why the data in question doesn't exist, what approach you are taking to identify the benefits of the learning program, and then move on. Don't try to fudge it or dance around the issue. It's better to stare that bully down immediately than run from it through an entire presentation. It's much more professional and much more responsible, too. Such a statement also reinforces your credibility as an honest reporter of organizational health and prevents you from making claims or promises you can't deliver or substantiate.

Other Types of Value

Another intangible that learning professionals deal with regularly is the issue of value. Definitions of value are many and varied, but one idea that can serve learning professionals in a number of different ways is the notion that value in the marketplace is largely determined by the customer. In the case of learning and development, the customers are line managers and other employees whom the training is supposed to help. Employees know more about their individual jobs than anyone else does, so when they say they have received some positive benefit— that is, value—from training, one can presume that this benefit will help them do their jobs better.

Organizations reap benefits from intangibles such as better morale and greater loyalty among employees who perceive the value of training, but companies that have a large engineering or technical component derive another benefit from employee satisfaction. With the looming retirement of baby boomers and the resultant scramble for talent, companies must not only retain their employee talent, but also must be able to compete successfully with thousands of other companies who are also looking for the top-notch people. Good employees shop for jobs the way they shop for a car, looking for the most features and benefits they can get for the money, so employers have to treat top talent like top customers. They have to start making a conscious effort to offer as much value as they can to the people who represent the future of their enterprise. Otherwise, they will fall behind.

Granted, most organizations do not think this way now, but they are starting to, and stellar training is an important linchpin. As the pool of viable candidates dwindles and as job functions become more specialized, particularly in the areas of research and development where innovative thinking is critical, even the best job candidates are unlikely to have the sort of experience and training a company like Genentech, Pfizer, or Microsoft needs. Such companies are creating their own graduate-level learning institutions to impart the knowledge that their workers need. Conventional colleges and universities can't supply the specialized knowledge required by these organizations, so the university's job in our society is increasingly becoming that of intellectual midwife: bringing students just far enough along into the world that they can survive and letting corporations take over after that. Over the next 20 or so years, this trend will mean that the demands and expectations on the training function are going to increase, along with its overall value and contribution to the enterprise.

The "So What" Factor

In the short term, if you need to add some tangibility to your argument, your best tactic is to paint a picture of the benefits of implementing your initiative or a picture of what will happen if they *don't* implement it. Tony Jeary calls this approach the "So What" factor.

In principle, "The So What Factor" describes a state of mind that is prevalent most of the time in any audience, no matter how large or small (Jeary & Magnacca, 2006). In that state of mind, while a presenter is speaking, those in the audience are continually asking themselves: "So what does that mean to me?" As a presenter, this is one of the primary questions you need to answer or your presentation isn't likely to make much of an impression.

CEOs are just like everyone else in this regard, except that their tolerance for irrelevant information is much lower. If anything, senior executives ask, "What does it mean for me?" with even more urgency than other people.

"Why are you telling me this?" "Why should I care?" "What's in it for me?" All these questions are all variants of the "so what" factor. To counter this state of mind, you must consider several points, including how well you know the executives you are speaking to and how thoroughly you understand the issues that drive them. Again, this comes back to the core ideas of Presentation Mastery: knowing your audience well enough to recognize what's important to them, how they want their information delivered, and how they are likely to respond to various types of information you present, both positive and negative. The "So What" factor should remind you that what's perceived as a good thing for one person may not be seen as good from another point of view. If your proposal, for example, would take 20 salespeople out of the field for a day, the projected benefit may be worth it from a company-wide perspective, but if it is happening at the end of the month, when the vice president of sales is scrambling to make his or her quota, you can expect some resistance and, therefore, need to take his or her viewpoint into account as well.

The Power of Negatives

The "so what" factor also includes warning people of bad or unfortunate things that might happen if they make the wrong decision. The prospect of losing something can be a powerful motivator. Indeed, everyone in business stresses the importance of staying positive, but psychologically speaking, research has shown that framing arguments in terms of what people might lose, rather than what they might gain, is actually more persuasive. Consequently, when dealing with intangibles, speculation, or uncertainty, it's often more practical and persuasive to talk about what might happen if an organization doesn't invest in learning and development rather than what will happen if it does.

Incidentally, one of the paradoxes of learning is that everyone knows it has value because no organization in its right mind would eliminate it completely. Even so, many organizations seem more than willing to experiment with how little they can get by with in terms of employee training and development, somehow forgetting or choosing to ignore that all cuts have consequences. Among the consequences of cutting learning budgets is a raft of hidden costs that decision makers need to consider:

- *Lost productivity:* An inadequately trained workforce is one that isn't working up to its potential or capacity.

- *Skills gaps:* A skills gap is a significant gap between an organization's skill needs and the current capabilities of its workforce. Employees with the wrong or underdeveloped skills limit an organization's ability to grow—and growth is the number one issue for CEOs today.

- *Wasted time:* Ill-trained workers waste time trying to learn things they should already know.

- *Lost opportunities:* A workforce that isn't as agile or as flexible as it needs to be will miss or overlook opportunities that might otherwise bear fruit.

- *Mistakes and wrong turns:* Poorly trained employees make more mistakes, wasting resources and time. They cause inefficiencies that can severely limit the performance of the organization.

- *Lack of leadership:* Poor leaders make bad decisions, which can send an organization's resources spiraling in unproductive directions.

- *Customer dissatisfaction:* An inability to interact professionally with current and potential customers affects the bottom line directly by choking off new business at the source.

- *Missed sales:* There is a difference between good, well-trained salespeople and mediocre or bad salespeople. That difference can be counted in dollars.

- *Round pegs, square holes:* Organizations that, for the sake of expediency, try to squeeze the wrong people into the wrong positions pay for it in compromised productivity, low morale, high turnover, and the cost of hiring and retraining.

- *Retention problems:* Organizations that don't invest adequately in learning or in communicating to their employees that their professional development is a priority experience higher turnover rates at all levels.

- *Succession issues:* Senior leaders and all-star talent may abandon ship if they don't feel that they're being groomed properly. When they leave, they take valuable institutional knowledge with them.

- *Morale problems:* A workforce that does not feel appreciated or valued is an unproductive workforce. Remember that 80 percent of the time when people switch employers, it's not for a better job, it's because they didn't feel appreciated.

It doesn't matter what the proposal is, you can always come up with a list of possible negative consequences for failing to act in one way or another. Unfortunately, that is the Achilles' heel of this negative-consequences approach. When going the negative route, you want to avoid coming off as a fear-monger or alarmist, or as someone who engages in scare tactics for the sake of manipulation. The tone you want to strike is that of a pragmatic realist who isn't afraid to face uncomfortable questions or, when necessary, speak truth to power. Furthermore, even though many of the things you are talking about may be unpleasant to contemplate, you want everyone to know that you are only discussing it because you believe it's in the best interests of the organization to do so. Not coincidentally, before you raise such issues, you should ask yourself if it is truly in the best interests of the organization. If the answer is no, then our advice is wait until you can come up with legitimate issues for senior management to worry about.

Put a Number on It Anyway

Another way to turn intangibles into tangibles is to develop assessments for very specific things for which you want a number, but which don't lend themselves to other types of measurement. For example, presentation and public-speaking skills are something that most people would describe as intangibles that are difficult to quantify. For the most part, they include qualitative judgments about how well various skills or techniques are executed by someone in a presentation situation. If asked to rate a presentation on a scale of 1 to 10, someone might be able to narrow it down to a 7 or 8, but beyond that, most people would assume that numeric information about presentation skills isn't of much use.

However, just about any professional skill can be broken down into its component parts, and if those parts can be isolated and numeric parameters for performance established, it's possible to develop mini-assessments that can provide all sorts of data that's both qualitative *and* quantitative.

For example, a simple presentation skills assessment questionnaire could break presentation skills down into two basic categories—preparedness and delivery—and then further break those categories down into 30 subskills for preparation and 30 subskills for delivery. A person could self-assess on a 4-point scale, ranging from never to always, how often they perform such basic practices of Presentation Mastery as "plan ahead for materials and equipment requirements," or "prepare and develop standard routines for key recurring presentation elements such as openings, introductions, icebreakers, audience involvement, feedback, closing, and evaluations." Such an assessment would not require much time, but it would give people a good idea, based on the scoring, of which skills they need work on. Comparing composite scores before and after a presentation skills course, for example, could give an idea about how effective the training was in improving the learners' presentation skills and could serve as a basis for guiding the learners' development plans.

This same basic approach can be used to quantify just about anything, from morale and leadership issues to accounting practices and marketing techniques. It takes some time to break down a skill into its component parts, but that's the most difficult part. Once you have created an assessment, you can use it repeatedly. If you run into someone who wants numbers, not words, you're prepared. All you have to say is, "LaToya rated her personal effectiveness at 4, which is at the high end of basic skills level 1, but she scored a 1 on her assessment score, which places her at the low end of level 2 advanced skills. A realistic goal for her is to reach an assessment score of 4 within a year, which would put her on the cusp of level 3 mastery."

Working Backward

Finally, in the absence of impressive financial data from past successes, try shifting the focus of discussions to the future. After all, even if you have numbers to share, they aren't necessarily an accurate indication of what's going to happen tomorrow. And, when you boil it down, all discussions about learning and performance are essentially conversations about the future because the purpose of going over past performance and analyzing trends is to get a clearer idea about what lies ahead.

The future you envision may be substantially different from the future others want to put in place, however, and therein lies the challenge. For proactive learning professionals who want to operate more as a strategic partner and less as an order-taker, discussions of the future should also be considered opportunities to assert the strategic value of learning and development and should demonstrate how learning can help build the dynamic, flexible, responsive workforce that senior executives need to meet the challenges of the 21st century.

Tactically speaking, the true shift in such discussions is from *performance* to *capabilities*—from what *has* happened to what *can* happen. For example, in 2001, when Gamal Aziz was hired as president of the MGM Grand in Las Vegas, he walked into the hotel's most profitable restaurant, Gatsby's, and ordered that it be gutted to build a new restaurant. At the time, most people thought he was crazy, but four years later, in 2005, the new restaurant Aziz built, Nobhill, pulled in $6.5 million in sales, whereas the previous restaurant, Gatsby's, had only been doing $2.1 million in sales (Kaihla, 2006). Instead of settling for modest growth of 10 percent or so, Aziz delivered more than a 300 percent return on the same square footage.

Aziz is now being hailed as a miracle worker in the casino industry, all because he uses a counterintuitive and suspiciously straightforward process he calls "working backward," in which he calculates the maximum possible value a business can return, subtracts the actual earnings, and considers the difference a "loss," even if the establishment is technically making a decent profit (Kaihla, 2006).

Learning professionals need to rip a page out of Aziz's playbook and start talking seriously about the full capability of an organization's workforce *if their people were managed as strategic assets rather than as folks hired to do a job*. In most cases, that means thinking differently about learning's role in maintaining organizational health and implementing business strategies. It also means engaging the rest of the organization in a conversation about the sorts of change necessary to make strategic partnering possible in the first place, as well as consideration of the long-term challenges facing the organization and how best to address them. Obviously, these conversations need to include (and are preferably initiated by) senior executives. Regardless of who is talking to whom, the following topic areas can serve as conversation starters:

- *We need to develop more of our own data.* For an organization to understand the true financial impact of its learning efforts, measurable indicators of performance need to be established and agreed upon. The workplace learning profession has already developed numerous sophisticated tools for measuring business-level impact. Learning professionals need to gradually introduce more meaningful metrics into their systems and keep beating the accountability drum.

- *We need to see other people's data.* To identify skills or performance gaps and other organizational issues that learning might address, data needs to be shared more freely among departments. Cross-functional teams can't communicate if they don't share information, so data transparency between departments must be a top priority.

■ *Our people need to develop sharper business skills.* No one is going to take learning professionals seriously as business partners if we don't know how to read a balance sheet and if we can't talk to decision makers in their own language. Our people also need to understand how the entire business works, which means knowing how all the organizational departments fit together, as well as how power, influence, and knowledge flow through the organization. More people with formal business training, generally, and with master's degrees in business administration, particularly, would help.

■ *Everyone needs to know how to build a business case for learning.* One of the greatest benefits of understanding how an organization works is that it enables you to make a solid business case for learning initiatives based on the realities of the organization, not idealistic fantasies. Knowing how to build and present a solid business case is expected of those with a seat at the table. Those who can't do it won't be getting the respect or responsibility they seek anytime soon.

■ *We need to know what's important to the CEO and chief operating officer (COO)?* Any effort that aims for strategic relevance must start with a deep understanding of the top priorities of senior leadership. This includes but is not limited to the organization's strategies and objectives. Other factors it might include are the politics of the organization's leadership, the nature of the organization's bonus structure, shareholder pressures, outside market forces, companywide cultural issues, competing or conflicting agendas, succession issues, and so forth.

■ *Developing a consulting mindset, including analytical skills, is a must.* To behave like a strategic business partner, learning professionals need to know how to interact with a broad range of people, ask the right questions, listen intently to the answers, and develop solutions that are right for the specific organization and situation. These are the skills that a good outside consultant uses to bring value to an enterprise. Learning professionals need to develop and use these skills to bring value to the table as well.

■ *We need to create a comprehensive learning development plan.* To reposition learning where it can make a strategic difference, a development plan for the transformation of the learning function is needed. In addition to its own mission and objectives, this plan should be a capability model that includes specific tactics for achieving those objectives, as outlined in table 10-1.

Whichever approach you decide to take, remember that decision makers are looking for ways to improve their organization. They can't see every problem, though, and they don't always know what's best. Your advantage over a CEO or COO is that you're closer to the action and are, therefore, better positioned to identify problems and design solutions. If you can get them to see what you see, chances are that they'll nod their heads in agreement.

Also, remember that even though the CEO and the executive team are the architects of the organization's vision, they can't possibly anticipate all of the ramifications and consequences of their decisions once they are set in motion. Whether you're working inside the organization or coming at it from the outside, a big part of your job is embracing the vision set out by the CEO, and then, like a scout in a wagon train, going out in different directions to find out what surprises lie ahead. Two types of information have the greatest value in any long journey: information that will help save time or money, and information that will help avoid problems along the way. Be the bearer of either type of information and people will listen, especially if you can get them to imagine the future in ways that connect them physically and emotionally to the story you are telling.

Table 10-1. Tactics for a comprehensive learning development plan.

- Greater participation from senior leadership
- Definitions of new roles and responsibilities for learning professionals
- New alliances with other departments (for example, HR, communications, marketing)
- Identification of skills, knowledge, and performance gaps
- Informing all learning personnel about new ideas, skills, and methods
- Sharper business acumen and consulting skills
- More accurate analysis and forecasting tools
- Establishment of broader, sophisticated, and credible metrics
- Prioritization in order of strategic importance
- Overall management and leadership development
- Performance improvement strategies
- Process improvement strategies
- Mentoring and coaching
- Resource allocation
- Technology deployment
- Use of blended solutions for greater efficiency and effectiveness
- Cross-department data sharing
- Cross-functional bridge building
- Strategic outsourcing
- Embracing, nurturing, and adapting to change

Very Important Points

- Use metaphors and analogies derived from daily life to illustrate complex concepts or make connections that are otherwise difficult to understand or measure.

- If you don't have enough concrete data to support a claim or argument, be honest about it. This takes the expectation of statistics away and allows you to concentrate on the evidence you do have.

- Use stories and anecdotes to paint a picture of success with words and to illustrate subtleties or issues that the numbers cannot communicate. Stories connect learning to people but are most effective when they also connect directly to familiar financial constraints, especially the bottom line.

- Gather video- or voice-recorded testimonials to help make the human connection to people for whom learning has had a significant impact.

- Emphasize that the strategic value of learning is growing because of the competitive demands of a knowledge economy.

- Always discuss benefits, of course, but realize that it's often more persuasive to talk about what will be lost or what won't happen if learning initiatives aren't implemented.

- Use customized mini-assessments to put numbers on intangibles that are hard to quantify.

- Recognize that most metrics only tell you what has happened in the past, and most conversations about learning are really about what will or should happen in the future. Keep conversations focused on tomorrow's possibilities, not yesterday's disappointments.

Pinning numbers on intangibles isn't always possible—or desirable—but that doesn't mean that they don't provide value to the organization. This chapter highlighted some approaches to communicating that value. The next offers some practical advice that you can put to work right away to present your proposals and communicate in a variety of settings the value provided by workplace learning.

Presentation Excellence—Every Time!

To the Point

When you are engaged in a formal presentation, the great paradox is that on one hand you need to be fully informed and prepared with all the data and other information you need at your fingertips, but, on the other hand, you might have only a few minutes to plead your case, so you may need to distill all that information down into a cogent, five-minute pitch. Regardless of the length of your presentation, many of the same preparation principles apply. We'll show you how to prepare for both short and long presentations using a tool Tony Jeary developed called the 3-D Outline template, and we'll explain the eight steps to delivering powerful, persuasive presentations every time. Along the way, we'll also explain the elements of applicable elements of Presentation Mastery that can serve you well during such presentations, whether they last a half-day or five minutes.

B y now, you know that a majority of the elements needed to successfully present learning in any situation should be in place well before you ever start preparing for any formal presentations. These elements include

- deep knowledge of the organization and its politics
- thorough understanding of management's strategies and objectives
- awareness of how your own professional goals and strengths serve the organization's mission
- analysis of the practical and psychological factors that drive corporate-level decision making
- keen grasp of the business realities facing the organization (outside market forces, competitive profile, cash flow, and so forth)
- detailed analysis of the organization's learning needs, gathered through extensive interviews, various metric analyses, and other relevant research
- alliance of in-house champions and like-minded individuals who support your initiatives
- reputation for professionalism, honesty, and reliability, as well as a demonstrated desire to do what's in the best interests of the organization
- record of success to draw upon
- plan of action, derived from the expressed needs of the organization as understood from extensive interviews and research.

Presenting Your Proposal

At some point, you're going to have to explain what you want to do and how you propose to do it. Furthermore, you'll need to do it professionally and persuasively, in a way that achieves the outcome you desire. If you are a CLO or a manager in learning or HR, you may be required to present reports on regular basis. If you are a consultant, vendor, or executive coach presenting from the outside, you need to conduct such presentations when courting new clients or reporting to existing ones. Remember, too, that you not only need to be prepared to provide executives with comprehensive, in-depth explanations of your proposals, but also you must be ready to provide spur-of-the-moment, concise summaries of the same subject matter.

3-D Outline Builder

Whether you have to discuss program initiatives at length with executives or distill everything you know into a two-minute elevator speech, you can use the same basic technique to plan for either type of presentation. The 3-D Outline (Jeary, Dower, & Fishman, 2004) is a presentation planning tool that you can use along the road to Presentation Mastery. The purpose of the 3-D Outline is to provide presenters a clear, organized way to prepare for any type of presentation, no matter its length or complexity or how many elements (PowerPoint slides, video, music, and so forth) are included. Figure 11-1 offers an example of a 3-D Outline.

No doubt, you already have your own method for presentation preparation. Many people use a variation of the sort of I, II, III, A, B, C outline they learned in high school for writing essays and term papers. Although there's nothing wrong with that approach, it doesn't take into account that in presentation situations, many things may be going on at once. While you're speaking, for instance, you may be referring to a chart on a PowerPoint slide with a pointer in your left hand and gesturing with your right, or an audiovisual technician may be cuing up a DVD clip for you while you set it up with a short introduction.

The advantage of the 3-D Outline method is that it allows a presenter and whoever is helping with the presentation to see the structure and organization of the entire presentation on a single sheet of paper. The right-hand column is particularly helpful to assistants because it describes the physical elements of the presentation, perhaps some notes about the multimedia or reminders of what kinds of props, gestures, or

Figure 11-1. Example of a 3-D Outline.

Presentation Title:	Quarterly Learning Initiatives Update	Delivery Date:	9/12/2006
Audience:	CEO and vice president of HR	Start Time:	8:00 a.m.
Objectives:	1. Outline 3rd quarter initiatives	End Time:	9:00 a.m.
	2. Secure buy-in, get budget okayed		
	3. Recommend outside help for executive coaching		

| Final Preparation: | ☐ Make sure laptop and projector synchronize |
| | ☐ Get handout materials from Pat |

#	Start Time	Length	What	Why	How
1	8:00 a.m.	5	Opening: Acknowledge Bridgeman's 25th anniversary Tell success story	Rapport Credibility	Old-fashioned storytelling
2	8:05 a.m.	10	Overview: 2nd quarter recap: initiatives, numbers Overview of 3rd quarter goals Introduce 3-year development plan	Emphasize credibility, success Vision Need final approval	PowerPoint slides Run video
3	8:15 a.m.	10	Business case for development plan — Research, data, context — Competitive intelligence — Industry standards comparison — Our rationale: We're behind the industry curve	Ellison has been harping on this for a year; need to make him happy.	Hand out worksheet

#	Start Time	Length	What	Why	How
4	8:25 a.m.	10	Describe 3-year blended learning plan: — Online: Required preliminary coursework — Classroom in-house champions, subject matter experts — Fieldwork: mentor program, simulations — Contract for: executive coaching, leadership seminars	Never had a 3-year plan before; need to emphasize advantages of long-term outlook.	PowerPoint slides Run simulation video
5	8:35 a.m.	10	Measurement and metrics: — ASTD's WLP Scorecard: Walk them through it — Timeline	Need to align learning with strategic goals. No other mechanism in place yet.	Hand out WLP Scorecard sample
6	8:45 a.m.	10	Q&A and Summary	Going to take some heat on budget.	
7	8:55 a.m.	5	Next steps: — Work out responsibility chain. — Firm up timeline. — Ask for Thelma's help	Need to get working on it fast; we're already behind.	
8	9:00 a.m.	60		End	

Source: Reprinted with permission from Tony Jeary High Performance Resources, LLC.

197

voice inflections the presenter may want to use. The other advantage of the 3-D Outline is that in the crucial preparation time before the presentation, it allows the presenter to imprint a more complete, holistic view of the presentation in his or her memory. During the presentation, it can also serve as an unobtrusive one-page reminder for presenters, should they lose their place or forget what they are going to say.

A couple of other things about the outline are also worth noting. Between the "what" column for all the basic content of the presentation and the "how" column is the "why" column, which reminds the presenter about the logic behind the content and also connects the content to the objectives at the top of the page. The "why" column can also be used to remind the presenter what outcome is sought and what the strategy is for achieving it. For example, if the "what" is "to illustrate key market differentiators," the "why" might be "to convince Ed that innovation is necessary." Alternatively, the "why" can just be a single word: "rapport," "alignment," "inclusion" to remind the presenter about the significance of the information being presented.

The 3-D Outline template also encourages presenters to be conscious of their allotted time. Beginning presenters often struggle with filling their speaking time with high-quality material, but most people in high levels of responsibility don't struggle with what to say; they have a harder time figuring out what *not* to say because they know so much about their subject. These are the sort of well-meaning folks who try to pack 80 slides into 45 minutes because they're afraid they'll miss something, and halfway through the presentation, they start to panic because they don't know where the time went. Paying close attention to time is crucial, though, especially when presenting to senior executives. Don't go over your allotted time with a superior unless he or she invites you to. Among other things, not managing your time wisely is a sign that you aren't organized enough to stay within the established time limit, and it says to your audience that you don't respect their time very much. On the other hand, a crisp, organized, well-timed presentation sends all the right messages about your professionalism, so that's what you should shoot for every time.

Dedicate Yourself to Presentation Excellence

The 3-D Outline template is a tool for you to use in the fashion that best suits you. In general, however, superior presentations are a result of meticulous planning, sufficient practice, relevant content, and effective delivery technique. Planning skills and delivery technique are aspects of Presentation Mastery that people develop gradually as they gather experience and mature in their profession. The development of presentation skills can, of course, be accelerated and developed through coaching and practice. The single most important factor, however, in developing effective presentation skills is the desire and commitment of the individual. If you want to improve your presentation skills and make it a priority, you will improve. If not, you won't, and that's why many people have mediocre presentation skills at best.

The fact that most people do not make much of an effort to improve their presentation skills is precisely the reason why it pays off so handsomely to those who do. Even incremental improvements can pay big dividends, and making the commitment to Presentation Mastery as part of your professional development plan is perhaps the most important thing you can do in terms of the results it can yield per unit of time invested. As we noted in the beginning of this book, operating at a high level of Presentation Mastery means working efficiently and effectively to achieve extraordinary results. If those are the sort of results you want, keep reading.

The Eight Essential Steps

Our focus for the moment will be on the content of learning-related presentations, but as we discuss various content areas that should be touched upon when presenting learning, we'll also be pointing out some practical steps you can take to get farther down the road to Mastery. Learning-related presentations should contain the following information, in roughly this order:

1. Open with an appropriate introduction.
2. Outline what you're going to discuss.

3. Explain how you arrived at your conclusions.

4. Provide a persuasive context.

5. Describe your solution or plan.

6. Describe the timeline and metrics you plan to use.

7. Roll out your action plan.

8. Wrap up your presentation.

1. Open with an Appropriate Introduction

Your introduction should be tailored for the audience you are addressing. If it's just you and a few other people you already know, you may not need much of an introduction at all. Or, instead of focusing on you and your credentials, it might be more appropriate to dive in with a few sentences about why the meeting is taking place and what the goals for the meeting are. If you are not well acquainted with the individuals in your audience, you'll need to establish your credibility with a short explanation of why you're in front of the microphone and not someone else. If it's a large audience, ask the highest-ranking person you can persuade who has established credibility with the audience to introduce you.

Elements of Mastery:

- Memorize a 15- to 30-second elevator speech about who you are, what you do, and what your professional credentials are. Use it whenever anyone asks, "What do you do?" and polish it until it's second nature.

- Develop a variety of openings for different types of general occasions. That way, if you are asked to speak extemporaneously, you have something to say while you're gathering your other thoughts.

- Collect an arsenal of anecdotes, humorous stories, and icebreakers.

- Don't just collect stories; practice telling them to your family or a sympathetic co-worker who can give feedback on your delivery.

- Partner with a colleague and make a pact to give each other feedback whenever either of you is called upon to speak publicly.

2. Outline What You're Going to Discuss

To make sure your presentation starts out with a clear focus, state briefly the problem or issue you're going to discuss, what the hoped-for outcome is, and how you intend to achieve it. Ideally, this overview shouldn't be just a rote recitation of your goals; it should also generate interest by giving audience members reasons to listen and establish expectations about what you will—and will not—be covering.

Here's an example: "We've identified three areas where skills gaps are an ongoing concern. Our team agrees on what we think are the best ways to address those gaps, but there are some alternatives you may want to consider. Today we're going to discuss these solutions, and show you why we think our selection is the best choice. We've also put together some projections to show you how a long-term, three-year development plan would yield exponentially greater benefits than a one-year, short-term fix. Let's begin with . . . "

This approach differs somewhat from the typical speaking advice to "tell 'em what you're going to tell 'em" because your goal isn't just to summarize what you're going to say, but also to seed interest in your subject matter and establish the tone, pace, and direction of your talk.

It's also crucial to maintain direct eye contact during your opening because another goal of this portion of any presentation is to engage the audience members and make sure they're listening. If you lose them at the start, it becomes increasingly difficult to get them back as the presentation progresses.

Elements of Mastery:

- Memorize the opening portion of your presentation to free your mind for the more critical work of maintaining eye contact with your audience members, gauging their reactions, and identifying "friendlies" and champions who will help you along the way. Also, be aware of any potential "snipers"—people who may be waiting for an opportunity to shoot you down.

- If you can't rehearse your opening in front of a live person or two, draw some "eyes" on note cards or some Post-it notes and tape them to the wall or affix them to some chairs. Use them to practice making eye contact.

- Be aware of your body movement. Keep your gestures open but contained. If you tend to race when you talk, remind yourself to slow down.

- If you are presenting PowerPoint slides, stand to the right as you face the audience (to the left of the screen from the audience's point of view) because that position allows the audience's eyes to travel naturally from left to right and back to you, especially if there is text on the screen.

- Anticipate points of resistance that might arise and have answers ready.

3. Explain How You Arrived at Your Conclusions

If you are recommending a course of action, senior executives are going to want some insight into your thinking process as well as some evidence that you are taking all the necessary business factors into consideration. Establishing and maintaining credibility is important at this stage. Demonstrate yours by citing the business considerations that have driven your decision, how what you're proposing advances the organization's strategic objectives, and the business metrics that have affected your decision. For example, if you've identified a skills gap in operations management, explain the methods you used to identify the gap. (Are you taking the word of a line manager? Is there data to back up your assertion?) Describe the effect this gap is having on operations. Lay off the trainer-speak; use the language of business, and be as straightforward and candid as you can. Definitely let them know that you've done your homework, though, and that you are more than ready to discuss any question or issue that might arise.

Elements of Mastery:

■ We cannot stress enough how important it is to dedicate yourself to a deep study of the organization, its culture, management dynamics, history, finances, market position—the whole enterprise. It doesn't matter what your current position is or whether you're an employee or outside consultant, you can never know too much about the organizations for which you are working. Remember: To be a true business partner to the CEO, you must be able to see the organization as he or she sees it, which means knowing it as well as he or she does.

■ Take a course in basic business if you have to, but learn how to discuss learning as a function of business, in the language of business. Not only will you gain respect from those higher up in the organization, you will also make better decisions.

■ Demonstrate alignment by linking solutions to organizational strategies and objectives.

4. Provide a Persuasive Context

To explain why you think your proposed solution is the best option, it's necessary to put your decision in the proper context. This is where you get to shine by showing how much research you've done on what the competition is up to, how the organization's approaches compare to industry best practices, what the market realities and challenges are, and what your benefit-cost analysis looks like.

Your objective is to demonstrate how your decision fits in with the overall strategic objectives of the organization, as well as its potential affect on the organization as a whole. Obviously, if you understand the operating dynamics of the organization, you'll have more specifics to talk about and your rationale will be more convincing. On the other hand, if you haven't done your homework and end up guessing and speculating, the decision makers will know it and your credibility will take a nosedive. If you are asked about something and you don't know the answer, be honest and admit you don't know, but that you will make every effort to clarify the point as soon as possible.

Elements of Mastery:

- Do your homework: Know the industry, know the competition, know what strategies management is pursuing, know the pros and cons of their course of action, and become a student of all aspects of the enterprise.

- If you are an outside consultant, learn as much as you can about the organization to which you are presenting through annual reports, magazine and newspaper articles, and people you know inside and outside the organization. Remember: You can never have too much information.

- Strike up a relationship with an industry analyst or reporter who covers the organization. Call him or her regularly to keep abreast of what's going on in the industry and your competition.

- Keep organized files of the information you gather. The information isn't helpful if you can't find it.

- Work to develop personal relationships with key stakeholders, so that you know their viewpoint going in and are aware of their hot-button issues.

5. Describe Your Solution or Plan

Having identified the problem and provided the proper context, you are now ready to introduce your proposed solution or action plan. Depending on what personality types are sitting around the table (determined from the DiSC personality profiling system discussed in chapter 6), you should craft your presentation of this material as persuasively as you can. This might mean preparing your information in layers so that you have a concise version and a more thorough version in case a C-type personality wants greater detail.

Remember, the most persuasive presentation qualities you possess are your confidence and credibility, so make them work for you. Don't second-guess yourself or qualify your statements; be assertive and direct. As you lay out your plan, however, be sure to paint a picture to show what success will look like when the plan is carried out. How will the eliminated skills gap benefit the organization? Will there be any direct economic benefits? Does the plan save money, make a process more efficient, or cut out an intermediary? Are there intangible benefits that are important to mention? If other organizations have had positive results with similar programs, share that information as well.

Precisely how you go about presenting this information is up to you. The important things to remember is that most top executives are more interested in what the end results are going to be rather than the details of the program itself. Don't get bogged down in the minutiae of program content unless you're specifically asked. Instead, direct your energy to describing the many ways in which the organization is going to benefit and how the solution will make *their* lives easier and make *them* look good. This is where you need to be addressing the "so what" factor (chapter 10) in just about every sentence you utter. What's in it for them? Why should they care? Answer those questions to their satisfaction, and you'll get far fewer sticky questions at the end of your presentation.

Elements of Mastery:

- Memorize the DiSC personality profiling system and become adept at using it to identify the way people prefer to receive information. You can do this anywhere, with anyone; it's just a matter of putting your mind to it.

- It is often said that the 12 most persuasive words in the English language are "you," "save," "results," "health," "love," "proven," "money," "new," "easy," "safety," "discovery," and "guarantee." Practice using these and other persuasive words, such as "accredited," "certified," "successful," "effective," "impressive," "compelling," "high quality," and "superior." Use them until they become a natural part of your speech patterns.

- Remind yourself about the "so what" factor whenever you are talking to someone. Practice it until it, too, becomes an unconscious part of your communication repertoire.

■ Think about how you would present the same material in 30 seconds, three to five minutes, or 10 minutes.

■ Collect stories, anecdotes, testimonials, or any other material that's relevant to your initiative and can help you illustrate benefits and other positive outcomes.

■ Practice using metaphors from common life activities—sports, cooking, gardening, music, and so on—to help explain complex subjects.

6. Describe the Timeline and Metrics You Plan to Use

Having a firm timeline in mind, as well as start and finish dates, is important because it helps manage expectations about what sort of resources and effort the initiative will entail. Having these parameters in place also makes things that much more concrete and, therefore, more likely that your proposal will be approved.

In addition to a realistic timeline, the metrics and benchmarks you plan to use to measure progress and success are extremely important. You shouldn't have to guess at them, however. Before presenting this information, you should have already had detailed conversations with all the stakeholders in the process, including the appropriate senior-level people, to reach agreement on acceptable metrics. Either that, or the metrics you propose should be in line with what the organization already does. In most organizations, there is a continuous conversation going on about what to measure and how. Engaging the HR, marketing, or communications departments in these discussions is a good way to bring them to a wider audience in the organization. Find out what others are doing and learn what the people at the top want to know.

If you believe that more accurate and detailed measurements are required, gathering them "under the radar" is always an option. When you choose to share the information gathered from these efforts, make sure the timing is right.

If you have gathered any data or conducted analysis about possible bottom-line implications of the solution, this is the time to share it.

Don't promise too much; be conservative. It's particularly important to be perceived as someone who can be counted on to hit your projections. Whether your budget is set or has some flexibility, remember that, to the CEO, metrics are important as reassurance that the investment is being spent wisely and as part of the foundation for making intelligent decisions in the future. Anything you can do to help take the anxiety out of the decision-making process will be welcome.

Elements of Mastery:

- Gather whatever pertinent data you can. Try to get other departments to share their data with you as well. Transparency between departments is a goal of practically all learning-oriented organizations.

- Do not expect executives to understand or embrace traditional methods of evaluating training, such as Kirkpatrick's four levels. Acquaint yourself with other measurement methods such as ASTD's WLP Scorecard or other specialized scorecard methods that pertain to your specific industry or business and link them to organizational measures.

- Strive to understand precisely what sort of information your management team wants to know and do whatever you can to give it to them.

- Practice talking about both the tangible and intangible benefits of learning to individuals, to departments and business units, and to the enterprise as a whole. If you focus on intangible or "soft" benefits exclusively, you will lose a great deal of impact with senior management.

7. Roll Out Your Action Plan

Your assumption going in should be that everything you propose is going to be approved and that you're ready to hit the ground running as soon as you come out of that meeting. Toward that end, you should know exactly what needs to be done to quickly put your plan into action.

Ascertain who will be responsible for the various aspects of your plan and estimate the costs to implement your solution. You also should identify reporting milestones along the way as a means of accountability.

The main point to communicate here is not so much how and what you are going to do, but that you are ready and committed to doing everything that's necessary to implement your plan. This is not the time for equivocation or second-guessing. Demonstrate enthusiasm and confidence, and keep your doubts to yourself. If you've prepared well, your own doubts or misgivings should have been addressed already. Your job at this point is to emphasize that you have done your homework, you have developed the best possible set of solutions available, and you and your team are fully prepared to meet the challenges ahead.

Elements of Mastery:

- Make it your business to know the hot buttons of everyone in the room, and make sure your presentation addresses these issues directly.

- Know which roles you and the rest of your staff are going to play so that if someone asks you who is responsible for what, you'll already know.

- Minimize the number of unknowns. This will greatly boost your confidence.

- Be accountable for everything. Be prepared to exceed expectations and over-deliver results.

- Be prepared to start putting your plan into action immediately.

8. Wrap up Your Presentation

Before you conclude your presentation, open up the floor for a question-and-answer session, keeping a few things in mind:

- Ensure that you have ample time allotted for fielding the participants' questions.

- Look directly at the person asking the question and let him or her finish before you start to respond.

- If you are addressing a large audience, restate the question so that everyone can hear it.

- Answer the question as concisely as possible, but do make sure you answer the question.

- Maintain control of your emotions. Don't get defensive if the question feels hostile or threatening. Stay cool and answer as respectfully as possible.

- Never answer a question by saying you covered that information in your presentation.

- To make sure you've answered the question fully, ask, "Does that answer your question?" or "Does that help?"

- If someone asks a question you have not anticipated, here are a few possible answers:
  — "I can get an answer to that right after we're done here."
  — "I know what you're asking, but I don't have the answer at my fingertips."
  — "I can email you the answer this afternoon."
  — "You raise a good point. I'll have to look into that and get back to you."

Then, briefly wrap up the presentation by providing a quick summary of the territory you've covered, making sure to point out

- the problem, issue, gap, or skill set your plan will address

- why addressing the problem is important

- why addressing the issue in the way you propose is the best solution

- what resources will be needed to accomplish your goals

- what business metrics will be used to measure progress

- how soon management can expect to see results

- what success will look like when the program or initiative is complete.

A clear, concise, confident summary is the key to a strong close. It shows that your presentation had a logical beginning, middle, and end, and it provides a sense of completeness or resolution that your audience craves psychologically. Keep it short, though, because time is usually a factor at this point in a presentation. You want to make sure you respect your audience by not going over your allotted time.

Elements of Mastery:

■ Remember that questioners tend to convey how they want a question answered based on their personality type. Listen closely to how they ask the question and try to tailor your answer to the questioner's personality (DiSC) type. Study the following general clues:

— *D*-type personalities will often challenge you with questions out of principle, mainly to find out if you really know what you're talking about and if you believe what you say. Don't be intimidated. Answer confidently and directly, and maintain eye contact at all times.

— *I*-type personalities tend to ask questions less to get information than to draw attention to themselves. They are looking for attention, so make them look good by acknowledging how good their question is—even if it isn't—and taking the answer seriously. If you can be humorous, so much the better, as long as the humor does not belittle the questioner. The key is making the questioner look good, after which he or she will love you.

— *S*-type personalities often appear nervous or apologetic when they ask a question. Reassure them that it was a question that was probably on everyone's mind. Answer them gently, and make sure to ask them if your answer helped them.

— *C*-type people are usually looking for more clarification or information when they ask a question. They want to make sure your information is accurate and will probably want to compare it against other credible sources of information. If you can't answer the question to their satisfaction on the spot, offer to direct them to a website, send them an article, or put them in touch with an expert. You can also offer to find the answer together at a time of their choosing.

- Learn all the characteristics of the DiSC personality types so well that you don't even need to think about them. A good way to practice this is in meetings where other people are asking questions. Whenever a question is asked, make a mental note of the questioner's implied personality type, as well as the general nature of the ideal answer.

You've Got Five Minutes!

In real life, of course, one does not always have the luxury of time. Often, decision makers don't want anything more than a quick overview and some assurance that everything is on the right track—which is exactly what you should give them.

Short presentations are really no different in structure than longer presentations, however. The 3-D Outline template can be used just as easily to prepare for a short presentation if you have the time to do it, that is, if you haven't been pulled into a room with no notice. In many ways, planning for a short presentation is even more important than planning for a long one. The big difference between short and long presentations is that the primary challenge of a short presentation is figuring out what not to say.

Long presentations allow you to meander and digress every now and then; short presentations don't, so making every second count is the goal. A short presentation should be more like a summary: concise, to-the-point, and delivered with confidence. Short presentations need to include all of the same basic information about the problem, the context, the solution, your rationale, metrics, and a timetable, but you don't need to dwell on any one area for long. Break it up into three

Why Great Preparation Pays

Seventy-five percent of the work of presenting learning is not actually done in presentations; it's done in the weeks and months before and between formal presentations with decision makers. Presentation Masters work tirelessly during those interim periods to ensure that as many factors as possible are working in their favor. The payoff for such diligent efforts, when it comes to presenting learning, is that it takes much of the pressure off in terms of having to persuade top-level management to take one or another course of action. Much of the "presentation" is accomplished in the careful planning and subsequent successful execution of learning initiatives.

When Computer Science Corporation's Holly Huntley builds the business case for a program, she gains buy-in and consensus as she discusses the program with different stakeholders and listens to their needs and concerns. To the extent she can, she tests ideas in the field first, paying particular attention to cost-related data. When it finally comes time to brief other managers on her plans, she tries to be as straightforward with them as possible.

"In briefings, the less [learning and development] jargon the better," says Huntley. "Although some of our executives have picked up on competency language, I still have to be careful to put it in their frame of reference. When I started, saying the word 'competency' was a nonstarter, they had no idea was I was talking about."

At Johnson Controls, CLO Janice Simmons only meets with the president of the company once or twice a year to deliver a progress report and update on key initiatives. Although the primary purpose of these meetings is simply to inform the president what her department is doing, not persuade him to do anything in particular, Simmons and her team approach these meetings with diligent preparation. To draft it in a form the president can digest quickly, the department's annual report is distilled down to one page and, to avoid being tripped up or sidetracked, does not include anything the president isn't already aware of.

"We do all of our homework beforehand," says Simmons. "We talk to everyone involved and try to anticipate concerns before they come up. In many ways, it's just standard good client management. We go in prepared, because we don't want any surprises. It's the smart way to do it."

At Caterpillar University, David Vance is just as cautious in his preparations for meetings with the company's board of governors. He makes it a point to get to know all the individuals on the board as people and to discuss proposals with them informally so that he knows where they stand and how they are going to react. "I meet with them at least once a quarter," says Vance. "It's the kind of thing that takes time, but if you don't do it, you get out of touch."

Vance learned through hard experience that new ideas should be vetted before bringing them up in important meetings. "I've learned never to spring a new idea on the board of governors without first knowing how each person would react. Those dynamics are so tricky. One person can say something negative, and suddenly you've fallen off a cliff and you don't even know how you lost control."

---

basic parts, instead of eight, and focus the bulk of the time on the benefits and outcomes of your proposed solution:

1. The problem/issue and brief context (one minute)
2. Proposed solution and rationale (three minutes)
3. Metrics, timetable, and budget (one minute).

In the preparation phase, distill your content down into one or two-sentence essentials, and remember to deliver them crisply and with confidence. The "so what" factor should be your guide. Keep asking yourself: What's in it for them? Why should they care? Those are the questions they want answered.

Elements of Mastery:

- Practice distilling the essence of your presentation down into a single sentence.

- Most presentation experts will tell you that the most important part of a presentation is the first three minutes, but in this case that's more than half of your presentation! So make every moment count by maintaining eye contact and intensity throughout.

- Don't rush, even though time is limited. You can pack a lot of information into five minutes. If they want to know more, they will ask and grant you the time to respond.

- Be fiendishly organized so that you can put your hands on pertinent information in a matter of seconds.

- Let it be known that you are fully prepared to talk at length about any aspect of your presentation, and, of course, be prepared to do it!

- Be prepared to offer more in-depth resources if requested.

- In short presentations, your credibility, reputation, and leadership are more important than ever. Use the time to reassure them that you are the right person for the job and that you've got everything under control.

Very Important Points

- Great preparation and practicing the principles of Presentation Mastery take a great deal of the pressure off when you're delivering major presentations.

- Use the 3-D Outline process to organize both short and long presentations.

- Pay particular attention to why you're including certain information, and be sure to think about integrating physical movement and multimedia support in your planning.

- Keep in mind the eight steps of a successful learning presentation as outlined in this chapter.

- Use the DiSC personal profiling system as a guide to answering questions in the most satisfying way possible.

■ Don't skimp on preparation for short presentations. Even five-minute overviews can benefit from using the 3-D Outline format and giving plenty of thought to what needs to be said.

■ For short presentations, let the "so what" factor be your guide. What does it mean to them? Why should they care?

The Master Presenter's Secret Weapon: Passion

No matter how many presentations you give or how many techniques and tactics you squeeze into your toolbox, you must have passion for what you are doing and a commitment to excellence. That goes for presenters in any field, not just learning. To be effective, in this business especially, it takes a great deal of energy to work in a world of business-like efficiency and sometimes strive to overcome resistance to change. The only way to muster that energy day in and day out is to believe wholeheartedly in the value of what you are doing. Cultivate your passion for learning, and everything else will follow.

Passion is infectious. All great leaders know this. The bottom line is that energized, motivated, highly skilled employees are the best competitive advantage an organization can have. Belief in this truth isn't enough, though. To persuade upper management that learning is a strategic asset, learning professionals must build their own arsenal of actionable information, ideas, and tactics and know how to present their proposals in meaningful ways.

The principles of Presentation Mastery address this aspect of the workplace learning profession. Zeroing in on communication-specific learning strategies is a good way to find points of leverage that can be developed and expanded upon if the right people get behind them. Exercising the principles of Presentation Mastery we've discussed in this book can put you in an elite group of professionals—those who know and believe in the value of what they are doing and can communicate that value anytime, anywhere, to anyone, with the sort of passion that moves mountains and markets.

References

Accenture. (2006). *The High-Performance Workforce Study 2006.* http://www.accenture.com.

Alessandra, T., and M.J. O'Connor with J. Van Dyke. (2006). *People Smart in Business: Using the DiSC Behavioral Styles Model to Turn Every Business Encounter Into a Mutual Win.* Garden City, NY: Platinum Rule Press.

Bartlett, C.A., and S. Ghoshal. (2002). *Managing Across Borders: The Transnational Solution.* Boston: Harvard Business School Press.

Becker, B.E., M.A. Huselid, and D. Ulrich. (2001). *The HR Scorecard: Linking People, Strategy and Performance.* Boston: Harvard Business School Press.

Bernthal, P.R. et al. (2004). *ASTD Competency Study: Mapping the Future.* Alexandria, VA: ASTD Press.

Both, A. (2003, April 8). "Look Out—Tiger's Feeling Good." The Golf Channel. http://www.thegolfchannel.com.

CC-M Productions. (Accessed December 18, 2006). The Deming Library: Cultural Transformation Discussion Guide, volumes 24 and 25. Washington, D.C. http://forecast.umkc.edu.

Cialdini, R. (2006). *Influence: The Psychology of Persuasion* (Collins Business Essentials). New York: William Morrow and Company.

———. (2000). *Influence: Science and Practice,* 4th edition. Boston: Allyn & Bacon.

Colvin, G. (2006, January 25). "The War for Top Talent." *Fortune.*

Gladwell, M. (2005). *Blink: The Power of Thinking Without Thinking.* New York: Little, Brown and Company.

IBM Global Services. (2005). "Learning Governance—Aligning Strategy With Organizational Outcomes." http://www-304.ibm.com.

References

Jeary, T. (2005). *Success Acceleration*. Flower Mound, TX: High Performance Resources.

Jeary, T., K. Dower, and J.E. Fishman. (2004). *Life Is a Series of Presentations: How to Inspire, Inform, and Influence Anyone, Anytime, Anywhere*. New York: Fireside.

Jeary, T., and M. Magnacca. (2006). "The So What Factor." White Paper. Flower Mound, TX: High Performance Resources.

Kaihla, P. (2006, July 6). "Going From Good to the MGM Grand." *Business 2.0 Magazine*. http://money.cnn.com.

Kaplan, R.S., and D.P. Norton. (1992, January–February). "The Balanced Scorecard—Measures That Drive Performance." *The Harvard Business Review*, 71–80.

Kirkpatrick, D.L., and J.D. Kirkpatrick. (2005). *Evaluating Training Programs: The Four Levels*, 3rd edition. San Francisco: Berrett-Koehler.

Marston, W.M. (1928). *Emotions of Normal People*. New York: Harcourt, Brace and Company/Kegan, Paul, Trench, Trubner & Co., Ltd.

Phillips, J.J. (2003). *Return on Investment in Training and Performance Improvement Programs*, 2nd edition. Burlington, MA: Butterworth-Heinemann.

Rohm, R.A., and T. Jeary. (2006). *Presenting With Style: How to Excel as a High-Touch Presenter in a High-Tech World!* Atlanta: Personality Insights.

Rudis, E. (2006). *CEO Challenge 2006: Perspectives and Analysis*. New York: The Conference Board.

Saratoga/PricewaterhouseCoopers and R.W. Beatty. (2005). "Workforce Agility: The New Frontier for Competitive Advantage." Cincinnati, OH: Convergys Corporation.

Seagraves, T. (2004). *Quick! Show Me Your Value*. Alexandria, VA: ASTD Press.

Simons, T., with H. Andres and C. Petersen. (2000, February). "Multimedia or Bust." *Presentations*, 40.

Sugrue, B., T.O. O'Driscoll, and M.K. Vona. (2006). *C-Level Perceptions of the Strategic Value of Learning*. Research Report. Alexandria, VA: ASTD Press. http://www.astd.org/astd/research/research_reports.

Sull, D.N. (2005, September). "Strategy as Active Waiting." *The Harvard Business Review*.

Tony Jeary High Performance Resources, LLC. (n.d.) *3-D Outline Template*. http://www.mrpresentation.com/3-DOutline.

About the Authors

Tony Bingham

Tony Bingham is the president and CEO of the American Society for Training & Development (ASTD), the world's largest association dedicated to workplace learning and performance professionals.

Together with the board of directors and supported by a staff of more than 100 and a wide volunteer network, Tony focuses on helping ASTD members and learning practitioners build their business acumen, understand the profession's role in addressing skills gaps, connect their work to the strategic priorities of business leaders, and help their organization leverage talent—the most important asset in the knowledge economy. With broad-based business, financial, operational, and technical management expertise, Tony joined ASTD in 2001 as the chief operating officer and chief information officer. He became president and CEO in February 2004.

Tony Jeary

For more than two decades, Tony Jeary, known as Mr. Presentation, has advised CEOs and other high achievers to discover new clarity for their vision, develop focus on their direction, and create powerful execution strategies that lead to achievement and results. He personally coaches the best, including presidents of Wal-Mart, Sam's Club, Ford, EDS, Firestone, Samsung, USANA Health Sciences, and New York Life.

He speaks on his best-selling book *Life Is a Series of Presentations: How to Inspire, Inform, and Influence Anyone, Anytime, Anywhere,* written with Kim Dower and J.E. Fishman (Fireside, 2004). It has been studied, endorsed, and transformed into courses, videos, and CD programs in multiple languages.

Tony lives with his family near Dallas where he spends the majority of his professional time coaching and strategizing with selected clients in his *Success Acceleration Studio* or writing new titles about Mastery.

Reach him at www.TonyJeary.com, info@tonyjeary.com, or by telephone at 1-877-2-INSPIRE.

Index